Process Management
in Education

Also available from ASQ Quality Press:

Stakeholder-Driven Strategic Planning in Education: A Practical Guide for Developing and Deploying Successful Long-Range Plans
Robert W. Ewy

Charting Your Course: Lessons Learned During the Journey Toward Performance Excellence
Robert W. Ewy and John G. Conyers

Running All the Red Lights: A Journey of Systemwide Educational Reform
Terry Holliday and Brenda Clark

ASQ Education School Self-Assessment Guide to Performance Excellence: Aligning Your School and School District with the Malcolm Baldrige Education Criteria for Performance Excellence
Peter G. LaBonte, ASQ

Improving Student Learning: Applying Deming's Quality Principles in the Classroom, Second Edition
Lee Jenkins

Claire Anne and the Talking Hat
Barbara A. Cleary

Living on the Edge of Chaos: Leading Schools into the Global Age, Second Edition
Karolyn J. Snyder, Michele Acker-Hocevar, Kristen M. Snyder

Thinking Tools for Kids: An Activity Book for Classroom Learning, Revised Edition
Sally J. Duncan and Barbara A. Cleary

Permission to Forget: And Nine Other Root Causes of America's Frustration with Education
Lee Jenkins

Transformation to Performance Excellence: Baldrige Education Leaders Speak Out
Sandra Cokeley, Margaret A. Byrnes, Geri Markley, and Suzanne Keely, editors

The Quality Rubric: A Systematic Approach for Implementing Quality Principles and Tools in Classrooms and Schools
Steve Benjamin

Boot Camp for Leaders in K–12 Education: Continuous Improvement
Lee Jenkins, Lloyd O. Roettger, and Caroline Roettger

The Principal's Leadership Counts!: Launch a Baldrige-Based Quality School
Margaret A. Byrnes with Jeanne C. Baxter

There Is Another Way!: Launch a Baldrige-Based Quality Classroom
Margaret A. Byrnes with Jeanne C. Baxter

To request a complimentary catalog of ASQ Quality Press publications,
call 800-248-1946, or visit our Web site at http://www.asq.org/quality-press.

Process Management in Education

How to Design, Measure, Deploy, and Improve Educational Processes

Robert W. Ewy and Henry A. Gmitro

ASQ Quality Press
Milwaukee, Wisconsin

American Society for Quality, Quality Press, Milwaukee 53203
© 2010 by ASQ
All rights reserved. Published 2009
Printed in the United States of America
15 14 13 12 11 10 09   5 4 3 2 1

Library of Congress Cataloging-in-Publication Data

Ewy, Robert, 1940–
    Process management in education : how to design, measure, deploy, and improve
educational processes / Robert W. Ewy and Henry A. Gmitro.
        p. cm.
    Includes bibliographical references and index.
    ISBN 978-0-87389-757-0 (soft cover : alk. paper)
    1. School management and organization—United States. I. Gmitro, Henry A.
    II. Title.

LB2805.E93 2009
371.2'07—dc22   2009042937

ISBN: 978-0-87389-757-0

Publisher: William A. Tony
Acquisitions Editor: Matt T. Meinholz
Project Editor: Paul O'Mara
Production Administrator: Randall Benson

ASQ Mission: The American Society for Quality advances individual, organizational,
and community excellence worldwide through learning, quality improvement, and
knowledge exchange.

Attention Bookstores, Wholesalers, Schools, and Corporations: ASQ Quality Press books,
videotapes, audiotapes, and software are available at quantity discounts with bulk purchases for
business, educational, or instructional use. For information, please contact ASQ Quality Press
at 800-248-1946, or write to ASQ Quality Press, P.O. Box 3005, Milwaukee, WI 53201-3005.

To place orders or to request a free copy of the ASQ Quality Press Publications Catalog,
including ASQ membership information, call 800-248-1946. Visit our Web site at www.asq.org
or http://www.asq.org/quality-press.

Printed in the United States of America

 Printed on acid-free paper

Quality Press
600 N. Plankinton Avenue
Milwaukee, Wisconsin 53203
Call toll free 800-248-1946
Fax 414-272-1734
www.asq.org
http://www.asq.org/quality-press
http://standardsgroup.asq.org
E-mail: authors@asq.org

Table of Contents

List of Figures

Preface

Almost all of the 15,000 or so school districts across these United States want to improve. There are a few whose performance is so high that their goal is to maintain that level of excellence, but there are more school districts in the middle of the performance band who suffer from organizational arrogance, the belief that they are good enough and have no sincere motivation to improve. There are also a few at the bottom of the performance scale that have given up. But by and large, the leaders and staff of school districts—both professional and support—have a sincere desire to get better. Yet, the history of educational improvement is not impressive. With all the time and resources spent on programs, plans, training, and other activities that are constantly going on in school districts, there are very few lasting results to show for this effort. We believe there is a pervasive reason for the inability of school districts to improve that centers on a basic lack of understanding about how to manage processes.

As we will describe later in this book, managing processes is not just *a* key but *the* key to educational improvement. Unfortunately, except for a few isolated instances, there is a gap in understanding about how to manage processes that is universal in education. The reason it is universal is because it is not taught in educational leadership courses. You most often will get an EdD in education today without once being introduced to the concepts of process management. Statistics courses focus on understanding research results and hardly ever cover the field of statistical process control (SPC). You rarely find this topic discussed at educational conferences. The problem then is that educational leaders haven't been given the opportunity to learn about process management. This is the root cause of most of the failure of educational improvement efforts. Addressing this cause and closing the gap in understanding about how to manage processes is one reason we have written this book.

One additional observation: the U.S. Department of Education has developed policy statements related to what they believe to be the four major areas that need to be addressed to reform education. They are, "the adoption of rigorous standards that prepare students for success in college and the workforce, the recruitment and retention of effective teachers, building data systems to track student achievement and teacher effectiveness, and to turn around low-performing schools" (Department of Education 2009). Adopting rigorous standards, recruiting and retaining effective teachers, and building data systems are processes, and turning around low-performing schools would be a system of processes. Applying the concepts, guidelines, and practices related to process management as described in this book would create the kind of school district the Department of

Education policy goals are rightfully determined to achieve. Ultimately, success or failure in school districts is about managing processes, it has always been about managing processes, and it will always be about managing processes. The purpose of this book is to help you understand that reality and give you the tools to act on that understanding.

The book is organized into three sections. The first section is devoted to introducing the concepts and basic understandings of processes. The second section explains what we mean by process management, including the components of process management and descriptions of what process managers do. The third section is devoted to examples of process flowcharts. Flowcharting processes is one of the most valuable activities a process manager can facilitate. Our intent is to give the process manager a head start in designing flowcharts for district-level processes. The flowchart examples are not provided as the best possible ways to design processes, but as examples of what thoughtful professional educators and support staff can create when given the task of designing a process.

Acknowledgments

We would like to acknowledge all the staff members of Community Consolidated School District 93 (CCSD93) of Bloomingdale, Illinois, who have created, used, and refined the processes illustrated in this book. Their continuous improvement journey has provided excellent educational opportunities for children and improved services for all stakeholders. In particular, we would like to recognize Jean Weishaar and Carol Boyle for their help in organizing and preparing the processes and flowcharts that are included in this book. We would also like to thank Sharon Frys, whose effort to create and document processes has been fundamental to the success of CCSD93 and several other school districts using process management strategies. As her professional colleagues like to call her, Sharon is the "Queen of Flowcharts."

Special thanks also to Carol Ann Rush, who read the manuscript and as usual gave us some thoughtful suggestions for improving the book. Carol Ann was one of the first practitioners of the concepts found in this book, and that was a significant factor in District 15 in Palatine, Illinois, winning the 2003 Baldrige award.

Part One

What Is a Process?

DEFINITION OF A PROCESS

What is a process? Anything that gets accomplished or causes an outcome to happen in your school district is the result of a process. When leaders of school districts talk about making changes or improving something, they are talking about changing and improving processes. Processes are what cause the work to get done, so they are ultimately the most important single organizational function leaders must manage.

There are various definitions of a process but they all have common elements. *The American Heritage College Dictionary* (Third Edition) defines a process as "A series of actions, changes, or functions that bring about a result." Wheeler (2003) makes the point that "Everything we do can be described in terms of processes and systems. Taking an order, making an appointment—virtually every transaction we are involved in— are all processes." Steer (2001) says that "Every organization has processes. They are the sequence of activities that permit work to get done: at a high level, processes turn customer requirements into customer satisfaction . . . . Processes define how work gets done, in what sequence, by whom, and to what requirements." What these definitions tell us about processes is that they comprise steps or actions that need to occur in order for an output, outcome, or result to happen. Furthermore, the steps or series of actions that occur are purposeful; they are designed so that the output, outcome, or result fulfills an aim or a goal, or meets stakeholder or customer requirements and expectations. So a series of steps or actions that are random in nature can not be a process because whatever results from the steps or actions doesn't accomplish some predetermined end. Processes, as Wheeler and Steer point out, are ubiquitous; they are everywhere. Teaching a lesson, developing a curriculum, making a decision, serving lunch, learning a new software application, designing an IT network, determining a bus route, assigning a grade, developing a strategic plan, taking attendance, scheduling, making a menu, administering discipline, maintaining buses, cleaning a building, evaluating a teacher—even things like innovating, decision making, or developing solutions to problems—are all examples of processes. Systems consist of larger groupings of related or interconnected processes. Try to think of something you do or something that is done in your school district that isn't a process. See what we mean?

Clearly, understanding how to manage processes has to be at the top of any educational professional's list of skills and abilities. Then why isn't it?

WHY IS PROCESS MANAGEMENT SO IMPORTANT?

Answering this question requires a deep understanding of processes and how they behave. When confronted with the need to improve processes, leaders/managers at the district and school levels basically have two choices: they can improve the skills that people use when they work or they can improve the processes that direct people how to do the work. Which is the better choice? Juran (1998) calculated the percentage that each contributes to the cause of a poor result. He calculated that at least 85 percent of the problems are due to the design or deployment of the process and about 15 percent are due to the people who use the process. Deming (1982) calculated that 90 to 95 percent of problems are due to the process and 5 to 10 percent due to the abilities and skills of the people who work in the process. Bob Galvin, the CEO of Motorola at that time, asked Frank Caplin if what Deming said was true. Caplin said, "It's an underestimate" (in a conversation between Ed Bales of Motorola International and Dr. John Conyers, superintendent of District 15 in Palatine, Illinois).

The point is that the component parts of systems, called processes, are almost always the issue or problem when something is not working according to expectations. Designing, measuring, deploying, and improving processes will produce a much better result than focusing on the people who work in the processes. This is not what usually occurs. The fact that education leaders and managers are not skilled or knowledgeable about how to manage processes is one issue. Another issue is a predisposition to blame people who work in the process as the cause for any process failure.

For example, at a recent meeting, school board members were perplexed by the achievement gap between different socioeconomic groups of students. The conversation turned immediately to bad teachers and why they aren't being fired because that had to be the cause of the achievement gap problem. The more they talked about bad teachers, the more frustrated they got because they didn't think the administration was doing enough to get rid of them.

Assuming that there really were bad teachers and that these board member comments were not just opinions stated as fact, the discussion never touched the issues of why those bad teachers were hired in the first place (a process), why orientation and staff development programs didn't improve their teaching effectiveness (another process), why, as we found out later, over 80 percent of the teaching staff was rated as excellent and no teacher was rated unsatisfactory when they were evaluated (another process), why principals hadn't set up coaching or mentoring programs to help those teachers perceived to be bad (another process), or why these bad teachers had been tolerated for years and years (policy).

During this conversation there was never a suggestion by the superintendent or any board member that their time could be better spent on determining the root cause of the achievement gap to find out if bad teachers really were the cause of the problem. (No data related to the issue were ever addressed as part of the discussion, only opinion.)

It is this automatic reflex by many in education to blame people as the causes of insufficient performance that needs to be addressed. Blaming people should be the last response to gaps in performance, not the first. Had the superintendent or other administrators at the board meeting been versed in process management, there would have been a vastly different and more productive conversation about this very real and tragic problem. They would have understood that the results teachers are able to achieve are always constrained by the processes (curriculum, instruction, assessment, and so on) imposed by the district, and that the first suspects in these instances are processes, not teachers.

The Baldrige Criteria, considered to be a consensus worldwide definition of organizational excellence (Blazey 2009), devotes one of its seven categories to process management. "The Process Management Category examines how your organization designs its work systems and how it designs, manages, and improves its key processes for implementing those work systems to deliver student and stakeholder value and achieve organizational success and sustainability" (2009–10 Baldrige Criteria). The Criteria asks you to identify your key work processes and then presents a number of questions to determine how well you are managing those key work processes. For example, a school district might list its key work processes as shown in Figure 1.

The Baldrige Criteria asks if these key work processes are clearly defined, if the processes have gone through a rigorous design stage, if the processes have been thoroughly deployed where appropriate, and if the processes have gone through improvement cycles, reinforcing the principle that nothing is perfect and there are always opportunities for improvement. There is no magic list of key work processes, so your list may be different. Some schools, for example, would include certain support processes in this list. The most recent Baldrige Award winner in education, the Iredell–Statesville Schools in North Carolina, listed the design, development, and deployment of instructional guides, predictive assessments, professional learning communities, dropout prevention strategies, budgeting and allocation, facilities, and two-way communication as their key work processes. The point is that in order to meet the expectations of a major category in the Baldrige Criteria, key work processes have to be identified based on their contribution to the overall success of the school district and to the achievement of the district's mission and then managed as though the organization's life depended on them, which it does. Category six of the Baldrige Criteria is a clear statement recognizing the importance of

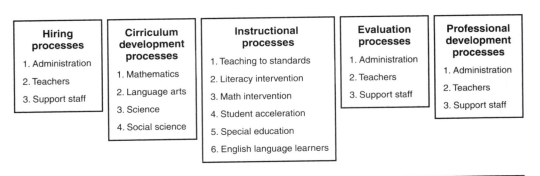

Figure 1   Key district mission-critical processes.

process management and its role in the success or failure of a school district. It is a telling sign that this category is often the most difficult of the seven categories for school districts to respond to when writing a state- or national-level Baldrige application. In most cases this is because key processes are not managed as the Criteria describe, and that is because school districts do not make it a priority to develop the knowledge or skills to manage processes well.

WHY PROCESS MANAGEMENT HAS BEEN NEGLECTED IN EDUCATION

There are of course many reasons for the almost total misunderstanding in education about process management, some of which we briefly described in the preface. A recent major education publication had a lead article that was a great illustration of this misunderstanding.

The article starts with a description of a problem, in this case mathematics achievement. Math achievement wasn't comparable to levels of achievement in other subject areas, causing the "problem." The next major section of the article described an interest an administrator had in a currently popular approach to improvement, one that he had learned about from a recently attended conference. They decided to "try" that approach to solve their math problem. The usual training went on to implement the program solution, and after a period of time some improvements were noted in math achievement. The article never numerically described how much the gap was closed. Everyone in the district was self-congratulatory, and the article ended with a "try it you will like it" recommendation.

The article approaches solving the mathematics achievement gap problem as a program to be changed and not a process to be improved. The committee immediately jumped to a solution—in this case the program the conference-attending administrator thought was impressive—before doing a thorough analysis of the problem. There was no attempt to address the achievement problem as a process issue, to determine if the performance gap was the cause of common or special variation (these two kinds of variation will be discussed later in the book), to flowchart the process, to analyze why the process was achieving the result, and to determine if the performance gap was caused by a process design problem or an implementation issue. The article is another illustration of a program solution looking for a process problem. (See the "How to improve currently existing educational processes" flowchart on page 45 as an illustration of this design or implementation issue.) Major educational publications repeat this scenario time and time again, which speaks directly to the need for the development of knowledge, understanding, and skills in how processes work and what needs to be done in order to improve them.

Another set of problems related to the acceptance of the process approach to improvement is best described in the book, *We Don't Make Widgets: Overcoming the Myths That Keep Government from Radically Improving* (Miller 2006). The book clearly and humorously discusses three myths that keep government service organizations (for example, tax collecting or licensing cars and drivers) from improving. The author, Ken Miller, states that government employees don't take too kindly to the notion of process improvement because they believe they don't make widgets, that is, they don't create a tangible product, don't have customers, and are not there to make a profit—all justifications for not using what they would describe as a "business" approach to improvement.

The same myths Miller found to be held by government service employees are found in similar rationalizations from educational administrators and staff. The "we don't make widgets" comment is repeated time and time again to justify using the current ineffective approach to educational process improvement.

PROCESS VARIATION IS THE ISSUE

Throughout this book we will be repeating the argument that determining if a process is successful depends on two things: achieving an increase or decrease (whichever way the target points) in average performance and a decrease in the variation within the process. More importantly, we will argue that variation is the more significant of these two measures of process success.

Generally, little attention is paid to process variation by senior leaders unless it creates a crisis, which of course the achievement gap has for many school districts across the nation. Ask a school district leader if they have set process variation limits for the core mission-critical processes under their responsibility and use that information to determine how well processes are working. Specifically, have they set limits or targets on the amount of acceptable variation in student achievement within subject areas? We predict that you will be greeted with silence. To illustrate the point, when was the last time you heard a superintendent or district leader say something like, "Everything we do that determines how well students succeed occurs in a system of interconnected processes, unacceptable variation exists in all those processes, and our key to successfully educate all students and close the achievement gap is to understand and reduce that variation" (paraphrased from the ASQ blog home page on Statistical Thinking to Improve Quality)? Yet, we assert that what makes the lives of people who work in a school district happy or stress-filled has much more to do with process variation than process averages. Variation is more often the cause of complaints from parents than mean performance levels. The customers of processes usually do not feel means or averages unless they are extreme; they feel and react to variation. What is the current emphasis on the achievement gap but a perfect example of school district customers (state and national as well as local) reacting to the variation in academic achievement between and among different groups of students? It has been said by Deming (2000), and rightfully so, that variation is the enemy. Yet this isn't the way most administrators think when they consider how to improve something in their district.

There are usually thousands of ways that variation can creep into the application of a process unless the process has been carefully designed, measured, deployed, and improved. It takes constant vigilance by the process manager or a group of people who have expert knowledge in the use of the process to monitor variation over time. Think, for example, of a teacher evaluation process. How can variation creep into that process, making it unstable? We asked 19 principals to flowchart the formative teacher evaluation process in our district. We received 19 different flowcharts, indicating that the formative evaluation process was unstable or unpredictable, meaning that a teacher in one school would not be evaluated in the same way (principals using the same process) as a teacher in another school. In this case, the instability of this evaluation process also caused it to be not capable. The teacher evaluation process would be capable if it were able to distinguish between good and poor teaching. The more complex the process, the more opportunities for the process to not be applied as designed, thereby causing the process to be unstable.

Educators focus mostly on means or averages because that is what they were taught. Variation is rarely calculated or discussed. To paraphrase Deming (1982), if you are focusing only on the mean and not on variation, then all you are doing is "tinkering" with process improvement. Understanding the importance of variation forces you to look at it, and that's a good thing because it requires a deeper analysis of why the process is causing variation and it also leads to much better hypotheses about what to do to reduce process variation and therefore improve the result.

Process variation is not unique just to education; it exists in all sectors as evidenced by the following quote. "We try to drive out variation wherever we can," says Charles Harper, a neurologist who oversees Mayo's clinical practice in Rochester. "Practicing medicine is not the same as building Toyotas, but you can still standardize. Uncertainty shouldn't be an excuse to ignore data" (*Time,* June 29, 2009).

PROCESSES EXHIBIT TWO TYPES OF BEHAVIOR

There is a precise language that has developed around the concept of process management that must be understood in order to be able to manage processes effectively and efficiently. The rest of the world talks about managing processes by saying that processes exhibit two types of behavior:

- The first is how *stable* (predictable, routine, common) or unstable (unpredictable, exceptional, special) the process is

- The second is how *capable* the process is in meeting or exceeding desired levels of performance targets or goals

Processes are either stable or not and capable or not. The two most important things a process manager wants processes to do are to be stable and capable. The process manager wants processes to be stable and capable before making them more efficient. Trying to make a process more efficient before it is stable and capable is just a waste of time and resources.

A stable process means that the process will achieve the same result over and over again. Stable (predictable, routine, common, normal) means that the people using the process find that it creates very little variation (remember that the best-designed processes will always create some variation, even if it is hardly evident) and the process users can predict how much variation it will cause each time it is used. If the people who use the process stay true to how the process is designed, it will have a very predictable range of variation. It can be used with a great deal of confidence that it will work the same way time after time. This process rule is important because as Montgomery (2005) says, "Quality is inversely proportional to variability." Stated another way, the more a process shows variability, the less it will exhibit the characteristics of quality. High variability equals low quality. People want the processes they use to be stable, predictable, routine, and common. This is good. There is a cause/effect relationship related to this measurement concept. The more variation a process creates, the more Excedrin a process manager consumes. If you don't have a stable process, you have chaos, and we don't endorse chaos as an improvement strategy.

If you drive to work, you want your driving to work process to get you there at the same time day after day. We want our curriculum development process to create subject area curricula that produce the same exemplary learning results for all students year after year. We want our payroll payment process to be 100 percent accurate all the time. A teacher wants his or her classroom management process to result in a low number of discipline issues and high levels of student engagement in learning activities. We spend a great deal of time designing processes to create stability. Think of it in the inverse, would you want to design a process that creates instability?

The second part of our definition of what processes do is to be capable. If you don't care what result you get you don't need a process. But, what if every time the process is used, it doesn't create a result the end users (customers) said they required or expected? If this is the case, the process is not capable, that is, the process as designed is not able to achieve what it was designed to achieve. That's ultimately why processes are designed in the first place.

For example, a school district had a goal that 90 percent of the students would meet or exceed state standards in all tested subjects. When analyzing past test score results, the process the district was using to teach mathematics was found not capable of achieving this 90 percent target. Think for a moment about what this means. The district created a target—90 percent mastery in mathematics—but gave teachers a process to teach mathematics that could not achieve the target. This is not good, as any process manager will tell you. The resulting frustration this creates among users can cause very painful eruptions within the organization. Designing incapable processes does not lead to job security.

A capable process means that the process will achieve what you want it to achieve. If my driving to work process gets me to work in 35 minutes all the time (remember, we just said that a stable process gets the same result repeatedly, in this case it gets me to work in 35 minutes) but I need it to get me there in 25 minutes, it is stable but not capable. A capable process is determined by what you want it to achieve. In many cases, core process capability targets are found in the district strategic plan (mission, student learning targets, strategy targets, and so on) or they are set at the highest levels within the school district (board or superintendent cabinet). They may sometimes be set at the state or national level. This is as it should be because determining what processes should achieve reflects the expectations stakeholders have for levels of achievement or performance. That doesn't mean that the people who use the process don't have a voice in capability decisions, just that the final decision about how capable a process needs to be is made by senior leaders, the only people who have the information and perspective to be able to do that. Determining capability is almost always a strategic decision.

Stability decisions are made as processes are deployed (implemented) and as they are used daily by people who have been trained and are skilled in putting the process to work. Stability decisions are usually described as tactical, meaning they are focused on how well the process is functioning as it is being applied time after time.

What is the answer to the question of what a process manager manages? If we were on *Jeopardy* we would say, "What is process stability and capability?"

WHAT YOU ALREADY KNOW ABOUT PROCESSES AND VARIATION

You now know a great deal about processes and the variation caused by processes. To paraphrase an infamous secretary of defense, you may not know you know a lot about processes, but as you will see in the next few paragraphs, you do. You probably would not use our language to state what you know about each of the following statements, but we believe you understand the "gist" of each and why they are so important for a process manager's basic knowledge about processes and how they behave. These principles or rules about variation, like the first one that says all processes have variation, were developed by Hoerl and Snee (2002).

All processes have variation. This simply means that any process will always vary one way or another from what you want it to achieve. Think about your drive to work as a process. You know that this process that you have designed won't get you to work at exactly the same time day after day. Most often it will get you there a few minutes before or after the time you wanted to get there. Following a recipe exactly, which is a process, will still not result in exactly the same cake, steak, and so on, time after time. If you write your name five times, there will be little subtle variations each time you write it, even though the overall look of the signature will be similar. Even atomic clocks, which run by a process, vary by as much as one second every 2000 years. The point is, if it is a process, it will create variation.

All variation is caused. There are reasons why processes vary. All variation is caused by something happening in the process that you don't want to happen. Many times the causes of process variation are actually designed into the process itself. In other words, the design of the process causes the variation. Not intentionally, but nonetheless it happens. Sometimes we can identify what those causes are, and sometimes not. This is why identifying the root cause(s) of process variation is so important, and also so difficult. If we can't identify a root cause of the variation, then trying to reduce the variation in a process is simply a guessing game. Unfortunately, because of a lack in understanding about processes, guessing seems to be the approach taken too many times.

Variation can be predicted. "Predicted" means that with a great degree of certainty we can know in the future what amount of variation a process will produce based on past results. We can know how much variation a process causes by measuring it.

We have used the word *stable* in this book, but *predictable* means the same thing. Predictability is very important when it comes to processes. Would you drive to work using a process where you couldn't predict when you would get to work? Of course not. Would you use a process to teach reading or mathematics even though you wouldn't know what the resulting student performance would be from one quarter to the next? We hope not. Would you want a payroll process that caused anywhere from zero to 10 percent of the checks issued each month to be inaccurate? You wouldn't be employed long if payroll was your responsibility. The world operates on predictable processes. If you fly in an airplane, you want the pilot to follow very predictable takeoff, cruise, and landing processes. Read the newspaper, identify the biggest problems of the day, and you will find most of them are caused by unpredictable processes.

Sources of variation are additive. Unfortunately, this little rule causes managers of processes lots of headaches. This statement means exactly what it says. Every process will have problems or defects that cause something not intended to occur. Each problem or defect causes variation, and these are added together to determine the total variation of the process. This presents a difficult problem for the person who is responsible for managing the process because it is not always easy to identify the different sources of variation in order to fix them. In fact, sometimes it is impossible to precisely identify the sources of process variation. A process could have one problem or defect that causes all the variation seen in the outcome, or it could have thousands of sources of variation. When you see variation in a process, as this rule states, it will probably be the result of a number of problems or defects within the process that when added together create a big variation problem.

Variation can be quantified. This is good news. Variation is not a mystery; we can know how much variation exists in a process because we can quantify it using control charts and histograms. (We discuss control charts and histograms in the section below, Understanding How Processes Work.) Variation is not an abstract phenomenon— something we know happens but are unsure of how much variation there is—because we can calculate the variation of a process and come up with a number that helps us understand in a precise way how much variation there is and what that amount of variation is telling us about how well the process is performing.

A small number of sources of variation contribute most of the variation. This is even better news for a process manager. It turns out that among all the possible things that could cause variation in a process, usually, but not always, a few causes can be identified as contributing the greatest amount of variation. This doesn't mean that these few causes are easy to find and change, just that a process manager should always look to isolate a small number of causes as being the culprits of most of the variation found in a process.

Process variation is produced by both the process and the system used to measure it. This seems obvious, but from our experience, almost everyone treats measurements or tests as though they were perfect. "What amount of the total variation of this process is caused by the way we measure it?" is a question we have never heard asked during discussions about why processes are causing too much variation. In education there seems to be an almost religious belief in the infallibility of measures and tests. Teachers grade tests with little or no consideration of the amount of variation in student grades that is caused by the test itself. For example, we would venture a guess based on experience that the grades of A and F are usually the result of special causes not related to the instructional process, and the grades of B, C, and D are caused by the common variation within the instructional process. (Note: What we have just said, if understood by administrators, teachers, and parents, would cause a crisis in education as it currently functions. Grades are assigned to students as though the student was the only variable that causes variation in the teaching/learning process. In fact, the curriculum, teaching strategies, books and materials, homework, tests, uses of technology, and classroom management are major contributors to how much a student learns. They are all part of the teaching/ learning process designed by the district and the teacher. Yet when grades are calculated, the variation these process variables cause is seldom factored into the final grade. These variables are treated as though they cause absolutely no variation in what students learn. This is impossible because curriculum, teaching strategies, books and materials, homework, tests, uses of technology, or approaches to classroom management are not perfect. If these process variables are not perfect they will contribute variation to what students learn. We have already made the point that outcomes are to a great degree the result of processes, and a small part is due to people, in this case students. Teaching and learning is a process subject to the same rules of variation that we have just described.) The result of state testing is acted on as though the data are without fault and cause no variation in scores, even though we know that even the best-designed test can only approximate what a student knows about a subject. Approximation causes variation.

A process manager must consider the variation caused by the system used to measure the process he or she owns. If that doesn't happen, significant amounts of resources and time will be wasted on improvement efforts because the information being used to identify process problems is misleading, inaccurate, or outright false. How a process is measured may turn out to be the biggest cause of process variation and the most important aspect of the process that needs improvement.

Process input variation affects process output variation. Now we are back to systems thinking. This rule states the obvious, that is, processes don't exist in isolation but are part of larger systems. The influence systems have on processes needs to be understood if processes are to be effective and efficient. We all intuitively understand this relationship between processes and systems, yet our experience suggests that few process managers act as though systems contribute to constraining or enhancing how well a process works.

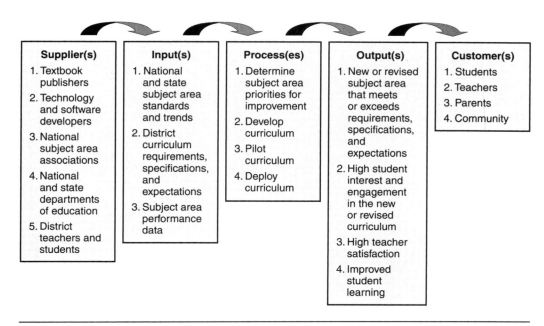

Supplier(s)	Input(s)	Process(es)	Output(s)	Customer(s)
1. Textbook publishers 2. Technology and software developers 3. National subject area associations 4. National and state departments of education 5. District teachers and students	1. National and state subject area standards and trends 2. District curriculum requirements, specifications, and expectations 3. Subject area performance data	1. Determine subject area priorities for improvement 2. Develop curriculum 3. Pilot curriculum 4. Deploy curriculum	1. New or revised subject area that meets or exceeds requirements, specifications, and expectations 2. High student interest and engagement in the new or revised curriculum 3. High teacher satisfaction 4. Improved student learning	1. Students 2. Teachers 3. Parents 4. Community

Figure 2   SIPOC diagram.

The most valuable quality tool a process manager can use to apply this rule of variation is SIPOC (supplier[s], input[s], process[es], output[s], and customer[s]). Figure 2 depicts a SIPOC for curriculum development.

Using SIPOC forces the process manager to think systemically. Suppliers provide inputs, inputs inform process priorities, decision making, where improvement needs to be focused, and contribute knowledge and information, processes translate inputs into outputs, and customers receive or are directly affected by outputs (George, 2005). By thinking systemically about curriculum development, the quality of what is developed is sure to be improved.

UNDERSTANDING HOW PROCESSES WORK

As you analyze the data to decide if the following two examples of processes are behaving well or badly, please keep in mind these basic truths about measurement: If measurement is necessary, then understanding what information the measure is telling you is essential. As a minimum, you need five kinds of information in order to understand current levels of performance, find gaps in performance, and improve performance. The five pieces of information are *center, spread, shape, trend,* and *results compared to benchmarks.*

Center information includes *mean* (the average), *median* (the middle), and *mode* (the most frequent). Their usefulness depends on a number of circumstances. The best thing to do is report all three.

Spread refers to the variation in the data collected. We have made the argument that spread is more important than center when analyzing data. The standard deviation is usually calculated to show how much spread, or variation, there is in the data. A control chart is designed to display this information.

Shape refers to how the data distribute themselves in relation to the bell-shaped curve. Histograms are a wonderful way of showing shape, especially if a bell-shaped curve is superimposed over the histogram. Each shape tells an important story to the person analyzing the data.

Trend data graphically display performance over time. Run, line, or control charts are preferred ways of displaying these data, as opposed to the frequently used bar chart. There are standard rules for interpreting trend data. For example, you need 8 or 9 data points to make any firm decisions about the direction of the trend. Runs of numbers on either side of the center point have specific meanings that are important in understanding what the chart is telling you. The point is, run charts are not easy to interpret. There are rules that must be followed if an accurate analysis is going to be made or in order for you to make sense of the data. (Examples of these rules can be found beginning on page 44.)

The fifth kind of measurement data answers the "so what" question. No matter what your results are, you have no way of knowing if those results are good or bad without a benchmark for comparison purposes. A *benchmark* is similar to a standard; it is a number that by consensus or outside review would be considered a target that sets a high achievement level. Fortunately, with the increasing number of Baldrige Award winners in the education sector, benchmarks are becoming easier to identify and apply.

Understanding How Processes Work (Example 1)

Figure 3 is an example showing data gathered from a process called my "going to work" process. In this case a single person is the process user, the process customer, and the process manager.

What can you tell us about how this process is working from looking at the run chart in Figure 3? This is a trick question because as you have already learned, there are certain things you need to know about processes before you can answer that question.

For example, you need to know what I want the process to achieve (When do I want the process to get me to work?). You will want to know how much process variation I can tolerate before my going to work process gets me in trouble. If my process goal is to get to work in 23 minutes, what do the data tell you about how capable the process is? What if I can't tolerate a 53- or 39-minute get-to-work time? What might cause a 53- or 39-minute drive time to work? Are the 53- and 39-minute results due to the way the going to work process was designed or to other things called *special* causes? How would I know that? What is the total variation in this process according to the data? What is the average amount of time it takes to get to work?

Here is the issue. If you want to improve processes, you need more information than what you have available in Figure 3 because commonsense reasoning is not a sufficient

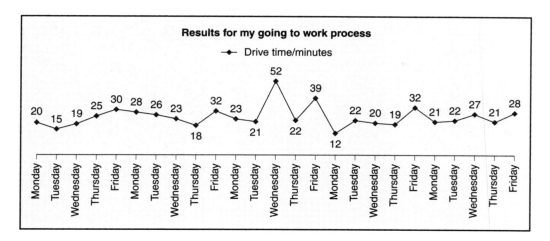

Figure 3 My "going to work" run chart.

or accurate way for you to answer the question about how well a process works. Arthur (2007) calls this "the foolishness of the five senses": "Your normal sensory apparatus isn't up to the task of finding and fixing the more subtle (and significant) problems that affect your job, department, or business. Like a doctor using an EKG or MRI, you need the right kind of tools to help you detect patterns you can not detect with the naked eye." You need to apply statistical reasoning in order to answer the question.

Let's go back to the original question: is this process working now that you know what target it needs to achieve? You can't precisely answer the question just looking at the data using a run chart. A control chart is necessary to answer this question.

Figure 4 depicts the same "going to work" data except that we have added + and – 3 standard deviations to the average time (CL) it takes to get to work, using an XmR control chart to calculate this information. Each line above and below the CL is one standard deviation. This issue of quantifying variation is very important to a process manager because he or she absolutely needs to know if the causes of variation are common or special. (Note: Shewhart decided that + or – 3 standard deviations from the mean would be a good rule to follow to recognize special cause variation. This means that if a data point is above or below the + or – 3 standard deviations line, it represents a special cause of process variation. Any data point between the + or – 3 standard deviations lines is considered to represent common or normal variation built into the process. He wanted to be able to distinguish common and special causes of variation but he didn't want to fall into the trap of either under- or overidentifying special causes. He didn't want a process manager to believe that process variation was common when actually it was special, and he also didn't want common variation to be identified as special when it wasn't. He based his logic on statistical probabilities but more importantly, on observations. He wasn't impressed that the statistics worked, he was impressed that engineers could use control chart calculations to actually tell the difference between common and special

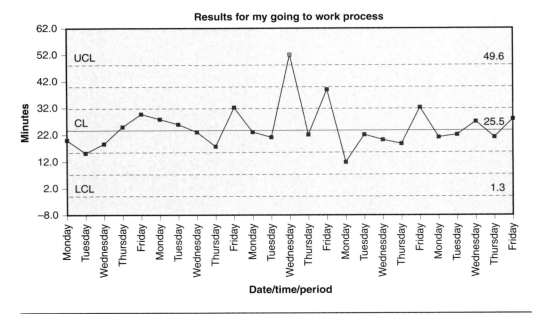

Figure 4 "Going to work" XmR chart.

causes of variation and improve processes. Plus or − 3 standard deviations means that 99.73 percent of all the variation found in a process is common.)

We stated previously that the sources of variation are additive, but this is true only if the source(s) of the variation is common and not special. The most important part of quantifying variation is to determine if there are any special causes of variation and eliminate them before calculating the amount of normal variation built into the process. (Note: Special causes of variation distort the true range of variation. Think of it this way: If you were looking at your monthly credit card bill and found a charge you didn't think you made, that would be an example of a possible special cause. You would understand that this charge would create an unusual variation in your month-to-month credit card average balance. You would review your receipts and possibly call the credit card company to resolve this problem. If it was an error, it would be an example of a special cause, and you would have it deducted from your bill before analyzing the rest of the bill. You obviously wouldn't add the special cause charge to your bill just as a process manager wouldn't add a special cause but eliminate it before analyzing the sources of variation in the process being studied.)

All the "driving time to work" numbers in Figure 4 are within the + or − 3 standard deviations limit but one, the 52-minute time. This tells us that the 52-minute time was not caused by the normal variation of my going to work process but by something special (a flat tire, an accident, unusually heavy traffic, ran out of gas, and so on). The 39- and 12-minute times are part of the normal variation the going to work process causes.

Now, knowing this information, how well is my going to work process behaving? You now know that in order to answer that question I need to identify what the special

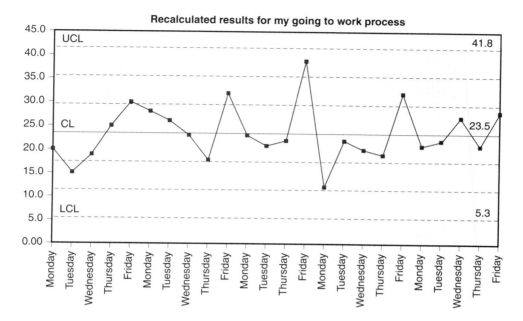

Figure 5 Recalculated "going to work" XmR chart.

cause (52 minutes) was and correct or eliminate it and then recalculate the numbers, excluding that one. The chart would then look like Figure 5.

The mean time I get to work (CL) is almost exactly what I want it to be, so the mean time of arrival seems all right. That is, on average I should expect to get to work in 23.5 minutes. The process is capable. Having common cause variation that ranges up to 36.5 minutes (UCL – LCL) day after day may be problematic. The UCL says that I could anticipate at some time in the future taking up to 41.8 minutes to get to work because my current going to work process has that much common or normal variability built into it. I have to consider whether I can tolerate that much variation in the process. If getting to work 18 minutes late (UCL – CL) might cost me my job, then I need to redesign my going to work process. If not, then the numbers seem to be saying that this process is working fine. The process is stable.

Understanding How Processes Work (Example 2)

Let's look at the next set of data and use what we have learned to decide how well this teacher's reading process is working.

Figure 6 shows daily reading test data plotted on a run chart for a six-week period. The data represent the percent of the class *not meeting* the standard each day. The average looks to be about 27 percent of the students in the class not meeting standards, and the variation goes from a high of 53 to a low of 18.

To begin with, are the center data (the average) useful or not? It's useful to know where the center is but not unless you know where the teacher wanted the center data to

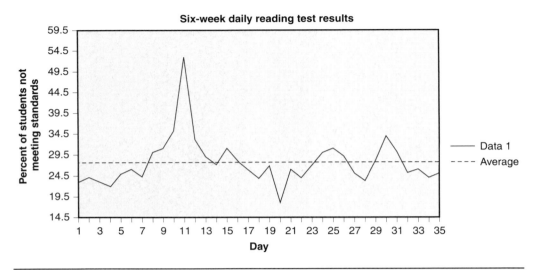

Figure 6 Daily reading test run chart.

be for this six-week period of time. For example, most teachers will tell you they want the center data close to 100, meaning that almost all students mastered the six-week reading content. This may or may not be realistic, but what the teacher expects or what the district targets are is important. Without that information, the center data aren't very useful because center data have to be compared to something, either what the owner of the process wants the process to achieve or some internal or external benchmark.

All you can say about the way the reading results vary is that they do, and some results look very good, and some look alarming, but that is precious little useful information. The quandary we have in analyzing these data is to speculate about whether the 53 percent of students not meeting standards on the 11th day is because of the way the students were taught or for some other reason. To use our language, is this unusually high number part of the common cause variation of the teaching process or because of a special cause? Unfortunately, a run chart can't tell us that. Actually, a run chart can't tell us much of anything about how this teacher's reading process is working.

The same data run on a control chart (Figure 7) tell us much more. We immediately see that the 53 number represents a special cause. If we discussed this number with the teacher, we are sure he or she would be able to tell us what happened that day (a poorly calibrated test, an unaligned curriculum, a tornado threat, a student illness, a special celebration, and so on). Knowing that a student failure rate that high is not part of the common or normal part of teaching instruction variation means that we can delete that number and recalculate to get a better reading of the common variation in the reading process. If the teacher can not identify a special cause, we would not recalculate but continue to look at the data over time to see if a number like this shows up again so that we finally isolate and determine special causes. But, please keep this in mind: They didn't name it a special cause for nothing; because it is a special event that causes

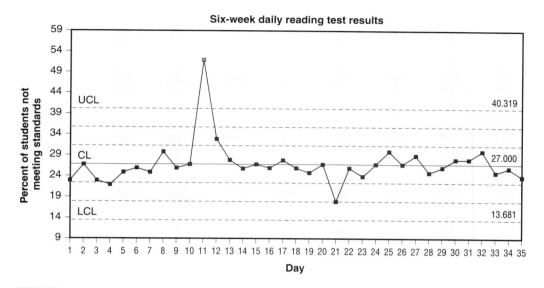

Figure 7 Daily reading test *np* chart.

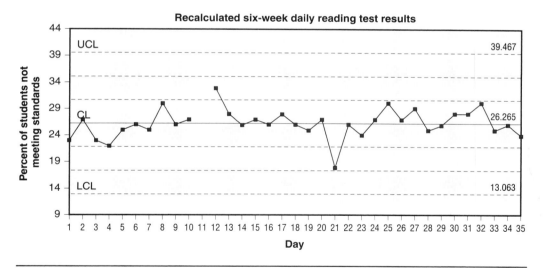

Figure 8 Recalculated daily reading *np* chart.

unusual numbers like 53 to occur, they are often easy to identify. Special causes leave lasting impressions on process managers.

Figure 8 displays exactly the same data we just reviewed minus the day 11 special cause, with a recalculated CL, UCL, and LCL. The CL, as we would anticipate, changed slightly from 27 to 26.265. The 3rd upper standard deviation, the upper control limit, or UCL, is now at 39.467 and the 3rd lower standard deviation, the lower control limit, or LCL, has readjusted to 13.063. This means that the teacher should expect for any day of testing that the students' average for that day could range from a low of 13.063 to a high of 39.467, all caused by the common or normal variation of the teaching process as it is currently designed and taught. What are the spread data telling us about how well this reading process is working? The conversation would then focus on how much variation is enough and how much is too much (Note: Even though Shewhart used precise statistical models and experience to set the + and − 3 standard deviation limits that determine common and special causes, you are not confined to that rule. You could, for example, say that the most variation we will tolerate in this district [or this classroom] is + or − 2 or even 1 standard deviation, applying what Montgomery said about quality being inversely proportional to the amount of variation found in a process.) In fact, in the example of the Figure 8 recalculated reading test data, there are no data points above or below the 2nd standard deviation, suggesting that the process doesn't exhibit a great deal of variation as it is currently being used, but we are sure the teacher finds that approximately one-quarter of the students not meeting standards is an unacceptable outcome.

We just looked at spread data; now let's look at shape data, using the same reading data found in Figure 8 but now in the form of a histogram (Figure 9). A histogram "displays bars representing the count within different nonoverlapping segments in the range of data rather than plotting individual data points" (George, Rowlands, Price, and Maxey 2005). A histogram adds up the frequency of each number in Figure 8 for us and displays those frequencies in ranges so that a shape of the data is formed for our analysis.

There are a couple of additional pieces of information on this histogram that need explanation. The vertical centerline through the top of the curve is the mean, which is 26.1. The left- and right-hand lines represent the lower specification limit (LSL) and the upper specification limit (USL). These specification limits tell us what the process is capable of producing. Don't confuse specification limits with control limits found in control charts. Specification limits are usually determined by the users of the process and its customers, and control limits are calculated when control charts are developed. Control limits tell us if there are special causes operating in the process, and specification limits tell us if the process is capable of achieving customer requirements. In the case of Figure 9, the LSL has been set by the district to be 10 or below, that is, 10 percent or fewer of students do not meet district reading standards. With an LSL of 17.7, the histogram clearly shows that the current process is not capable of achieving the 10 percent target.

What does the shape of this histogram tell us about how well students are learning the content of the reading program?

The histogram shows a fairly normal distribution except for an outlier at either end of the curve. The teacher, we are sure, would be able to describe what caused those two outliers and would also be able to suggest what needs to be done in order for the outlier on the right side of the scale to not show up again in the future. The outlier at the left of the curve may indicate a highly successful teaching strategy, one that might be used again with similar results.

The teacher now knows he or she has a stable but not capable reading process. All student reading performance results are caused by what goes on in the classroom.

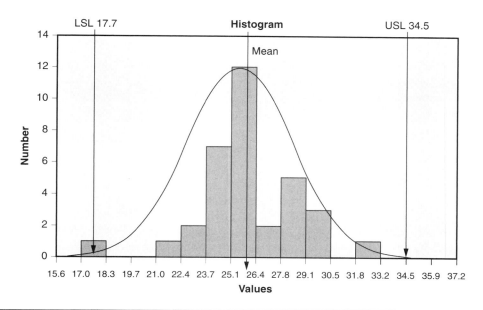

Figure 9   Histogram of daily reading test results.

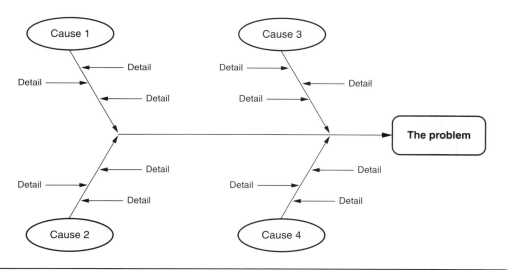

Figure 10   Cause-and-effect diagram.

Variation isn't too bad, but the average needs to be at the district standard. Improvement is needed.

A this point, the teacher might draw a cause-and-effect diagram like Figure 10 and begin to fill it out believing that this will help identify the causes of variation in the reading process. Our teachers are taught to complete a plus/delta feedback session with their students at the end of a unit or period of time to identify teaching strategies that work and those that need to be improved. Feedback from students would be a very useful source of information the teacher might use to fill out the cause-and-effect diagram. The teacher might discuss the results with colleagues, the principal, or district content experts for other ideas and suggestions. There are many online sources to find improvement suggestions. Using a quality tool like the cause-and-effect diagram organizes all this diagnostic information into an orderly exploration for finding causes of variation in the reading process.

Assuming the teacher continues this improvement cycle of data collection, analysis, and the identification and application of improvement strategies every six weeks, it is not difficult to envision that over time the results from the daily reading tests could look like Figure 11. You now know that improvement means the average is increasing—or in this case decreasing—and variation is decreasing. Reading left to right, the average percent of students not meeting standards is reduced from 26.26 percent the first six weeks to 17.11 the second six weeks and then to 11.46 during the third six-week period. Additionally, total variation (UCL – LCL) has narrowed from 30.75 to 24.83 to 20.31, convincing evidence that this teacher is working hard to optimize his or her classroom and create a highly successful student learning experience. In no case are there any special cause incidents that create havoc to the process. This reading process is under control and achieving increasingly impressive results.

Figure 11 is an excellent example of how all process improvement data should be displayed. Data are collected to show a trend, the data are analyzed to isolate causes of variation, improvements are made to the process, and then data are collected to see if the improvements made any difference. In the case of Figure 11, there are three six-week improvement cycles displayed in one data chart.

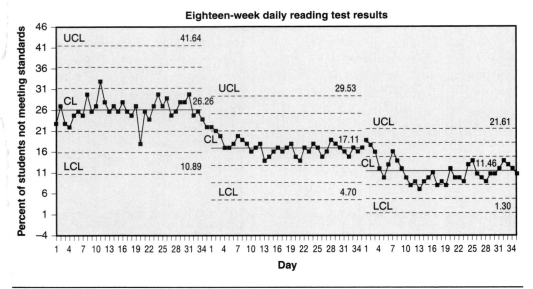

Figure 11   Eighteen-week daily reading test *np* chart.

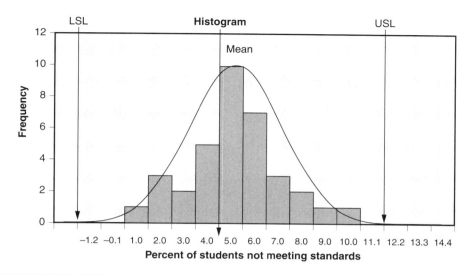

Figure 12 Ideal histogram.

If we extended these cycles of improvement over time, what would an ideal shape of these data look like after the teacher has optimized his or her reading teaching process? It would look like a bell-shaped curve at the very left hand side of the horizontal scale, indicating that all students are below the 10 percent does not meet standard. The Figure 12 ideal histogram shows a mean of 4.5, an LSL of 1 and a USL of about 12, showing that for this group of 35 reading tests, the average percent of students not meeting standards was 4.5 and that the process is capable of producing percentages of students not meeting standards as low as 1 percent and as high as 12 percent.

Any teacher would be justifiably proud of these results.

Understanding the information about process dynamics and behavior that we have presented up to this point in the book is a necessary prerequisite to being able to understand what a process manager does. Even though processes as they play out in organizations are very human events, knowledge about the technical nature of processes and how to understand what is happening when processes misbehave makes all the difference in the success or failure of a process manager.

Part Two
Process Management

WHAT IS PROCESS MANAGEMENT?

Process Manager

Certainly every mission-critical process, and arguably all processes, should have a *process manager* (sometimes called a *process owner*) who is responsible for how well the process works. It usually is an individual but in certain instances it could be a group of people. What the process manager manages is the design, measurement, deployment, and improvement of the process (see Figure 13). These are the four key components of process management that if managed well, create results that everyone is proud of, and if managed poorly, create frustration in the people who use the process, with results that embarrass everyone.

Process Design

Processes are designed to create an outcome or result that meets certain requirements and/or expectations. The process must be managed to achieve whatever requirements and expectations are stipulated by customers. How well a process manager understands this concept will be one of the major predictors of how well he or she succeeds or fails. This means that the first task for a process manager is to clearly define customer requirements and expectations. Most of these customer requirements and expectations need to be expressed numerically. What are the targets the process should seek to achieve? This

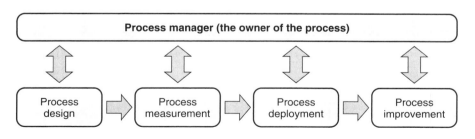

Figure 13 Process management diagram.

might be different for people who work in the process as opposed to those who receive the end product. For example, if the process is reading, teachers would be a customer group that works in or uses the process, and students and parents are customers who receive what the process produces. Each customer group can have similar or very different process requirements and expectations. The process manager needs to have applied very reliable methods (surveys, focus groups, interviews, reviews of data, and so on) for collecting customer information. The process can not be effectively designed without it. (Note: Understanding customer requirements and/or expectations when thinking about how processes work is critical. Processes, as the definitions tell us, are designed to create a specific kind of outcome or result. What the process is required or expected to achieve in an educational milieu can be quite complex. For example, designing a bus-routing process could have requirements or expectations that include the board of education's desire for safety and efficiency, the parent's desire for convenience, the student's desire to be on the bus the shortest time possible, and the principal's desire for on-time delivery and good student bus conduct. Furthermore, the bus-routing process designer needs a very precise understanding about what targets are in mind when the board talks about safety and efficiency, when the parent talks about convenience, and when students talk about the shortest time possible. Knowing principals, a target of no less than 100 percent on-time deliveries would be their requirement/expectation.

A curriculum design process would be even more complex. Customers of this process could include the board of education, principals, teachers, parents, state and federal departments of education, community members, and students. Each of these customers of the curriculum development process has ideas about what the curriculum should do or the results it should create, such as correlate to national curriculum goals and state standards or reflect up-to-date content area information. The point is that educational processes have multiple customers, each customer might have multiple requirements or expectations, and, in fact, it's highly likely that some might conflict. In our bus-routing process example, consider the possible conflict between the board's requirement/expectation for efficiency and the parent's requirement/expectation for convenience.)

Figure 14 is an example of a list of requirements a curriculum development process manager might have developed after meeting with various customer groups.

An additional list of possible requirements of different district customer groups can be found in Appendix A.

The process manager is responsible for the design of the process—the way steps in the process are sequenced so that the end result meets stated customer requirements. The tool usually used to design a process is called a *flowchart,* or *process map.* (Note: There is a distinction between a flowchart and a process map but it is a small one. We use the PQ Systems flowchart definition: "A flowchart is a picture of any process (sequence of events, steps, activities, or tasks) . . . drawn with standard symbols that represent different types of activities or tasks" [PQ Systems 1998]. The term *process map* is often used synonymously with flowchart but sometimes includes cycle time, resources, valued-added estimates, and costs in addition to the basic flowchart diagram.) This doesn't mean that the process manager has to design the process; this could be

---

State and district requirements

1. Correlates with board of education goals
2. Correlates with state standards
3. Correlates with professional subject area organization standards
4. Correlates with district strategic plan
5. Sensitive and adaptable to changing priorities
6. Reflects up-to-date content area information
7. Reflects research-based best practice
8. Tied to actual results: accountability (test and performance results or effect sizes)
9. Ongoing and preferably online evaluation built into the program
10. Not text dependent
11. Whole curriculum development and implementation process to take place during the school year
12. Includes collaboration with other agencies (that is, drug education programs, police departments, or other community agencies)

Parent and community requirements

1. Includes system for disseminating information to the community (including nontraditional ways for people of different cultural backgrounds, such as Homework Center, public library, translations, wide variety of media including video, e-mail, GroupWise system, local cable access, and so on)
2. Includes comprehensive stakeholder input (mainstream teachers, special area teachers, coordinators, parents of all backgrounds, nonparents, business people, students, high school students, and so on)
3. Includes high level of communication with all stakeholders during the development process
4. Uses community resources

Student requirements

1. High-interest materials
2. High and measurable academic standards
3. Real-world applications and assessments
4. Problem-solving experiences
5. Higher-level thinking skills
6. Socialization skills, including cooperative learning
7. Adaptable to different learning styles
8. Developmentally appropriate activities and expectations
9. Meets the needs of all students: special education (such as LD, BD, handicapped), gifted, second language learners, at-risk
10. Technology-based materials and learning activities

Teacher requirements

1. Involvement in the curriculum development process
2. Released time provided for development, training, and implementation
3. Clearly delineated research- or best practice–based activities, resources, assessments, basic materials, supplementary materials

Figure 14   Checklist for district curriculum development requirements.   *Continued*

4. Availability and budget for materials in different languages and modalities (and easy access to these)

5. Provision for ongoing staff development

6. Built-in new teacher professional development (yearly)

7. Written in clear, understandable language

8. Sequential, logical layout

9. Manageable format

10. Applicable to teachers and students of all levels

11. Integrated technology

12. Extension and remediation provisions

13. Adaptable for curriculum integration

14. Adaptable for multiage situations

15. Adaptable for special needs students (such as LD/BD, slow learners)

Figure 14 *Continued.*

done by someone else, by committee, or contracted to an agency. (Note: SmartDraw, Visio, and Inspiration are examples of software programs used to develop flowcharts. Microsoft Word also has templates to help draw flowcharts, but software specifically designed to produce flowcharts is much easier to use.) The responsibility a process manager has in this first step is that the design is developed by a person or persons who have expertise related to the content of the process itself, for example, by the people who work in the process. In other words, the process manager's responsibility is to assure that the process has been designed to create the result the people who use it require or expect. (Read the description of flowcharting beginning on page 39 for an example of how flowcharts are developed.)

Please remember that the way a process is designed will always create some variation in the outcomes or results the process achieves. The better the design, the less variation in outcomes or results, and the poorer the design, the more variation there is in the way the process works. This is why it is so important to take the time to design the process right in the beginning rather than implementing it and finding out it needs to be redesigned because it either creates too much variation or it can't achieve the outcome or results users require. That would be the way for a process manager not to win friends and influence people.

What we have described are two essential conditions to the design of a process. The first is that a process should be designed based on meeting or exceeding customer requirements and expectations. The second is that a process should be designed using a flowchart. If the process manager succeeds in meeting these two conditions, the process should create as little variation as possible in outcomes or results each time it is used. Customers want what they want and they hate (that is not too strong a word) variation because variation means that the outcome or result is unpredictable. A clear understanding of these two conditions is essential when designing processes.

Process Measurement

The reason process measurement is one of the four essential components of process management is because understanding how well a process works is difficult. Process managers can not simply look at data about a process and come to accurate conclusions based on commonsense analysis. One of the most serious measurement mistakes made all too frequently by process managers has been well stated by Harry and Schroeder (2000): "You cannot change the performance of an organization using results data. Results data can only tell you what is working and what needs improvement. If your organization cannot express how well a process is performing in the form of a measurement, you do not understand and cannot improve the process. You cannot improve what you don't measure." The problem this statement causes for process managers is that moving from results or lagging data (usually collected yearly like state tests) to leading data (collected daily, weekly, or monthly) requires much more data collection than is the norm in education. A general rule is that 8 or 9 data points are necessary to confirm a trend, and 20 or more are necessary to construct statistical tests that will tell the process manager if the process they own is working.

The usual language, as we have already described, that is associated with process results is "stable" and "capable," and they have very precise meanings. These concepts come from the field called statistical process control (SPC). That is why a process manager would want a measurement system that reliably collects stability and capability data. (Note: Statistical process control requires a process manager to know and understand the basics of this statistical way to measure processes because process stability is measured by control charts, and process capability is measured by a special kind of histogram. These aren't difficult statistical measures but they do require a level of expertise to know what control charts to use and how to analyze control chart and histogram data. The process manager will need to know the difference between attribute and variable data, and there are also some assumptions that need to be met about the distribution of data collected and sample sizes in order to use control charts and histograms correctly.) Wheeler (1999) says about SPC, "Statistical process control is not about statistics, it is not about process-hyphen-control, and it is not about conformance to specifications. While SPC can be used in all of these ways, it is much more than any one of these narrow interpretations. It is, at its heart, about getting the most from your processes. It is about the continual improvement of processes and outcomes. And, it is, first and foremost, a way of thinking with some . . . 'statistical' . . . tools attached." Control charts and histograms are the bread and butter of process measurement.

It is beyond the ambitions of this book to treat the subject of SPC in anything but a superficial level. There are some very understandable sources on this subject that provide the in-depth information a process manager needs in order to administer and analyze control charts and histograms. (Wheeler; Arthur; Gygi, DeCarlo, and Williams; George, Rowlands, Price, and Maxey; or Tague, for example) Better yet, many businesses have quality experts who are versed in the uses of control charts and histograms and are usually very willing to help a school district understand and develop the expertise necessary to apply these quality tools.

Process Deployment

This process management component would seem to be a slam dunk. The hard task of designing the process and developing a measurement plan has already been accomplished. Who wouldn't want a newly designed process that could make their work life much easier and more productive? Well it turns out that would be almost everyone. Change does not come easily, even when it makes the user's work life less complicated and more fulfilling. There is something about the comfort zone of the known that makes the unknown fraught with anxiety.

The most important thing to accomplish in deployment is to get what was in the designers' minds into the people who are going to use it, exactly as it was designed. Fortunately, the process manager has two pieces of information that help make deployment issues much less daunting and complex.

The first is that the new or redesigned process has been created to answer a user or customer need, requirement, or expectation. There is a legitimate reason for this new or redesigned process to exist. People who work in the process itself or customers who experience the result of the process have said that there needs to be changes. This is not just a process manager's desire to stay busy. In other words, there is a real, legitimate reason for changing this process, and the process manager has the data to make a convincing argument justifying the change.

The second is the flowchart developed during the design activity. A flowchart is a marvelous quality tool that displays graphic details about how the process works. It helps everyone involved see how the process is intended to work and the sequence of steps that need to be taken to successfully use the process, and describes what activities need to be accomplished if it is to work properly. It greatly reduces the confusion about what happens, in what sequence, when it happens, and why it happens. It is a great aid to anyone deploying a new or redesigned process. A competent process manager would not even consider deploying a process without a flowchart.

Lastly, the process manager must consider how work rules and existing procedures such as hiring, job descriptions, job evaluations, knowledge and skill training, calendars, policy, and other related activities are aligned or misaligned with the newly designed or redesigned process. These could become significant blockages as the process is deployed. A well-designed process that is misaligned with organizational systems is a deployment disaster about to happen.

Process Improvement

The last component of process manager responsibilities is an obvious one. Nothing is perfect. Everything can be made better over time, and a process manager should be focused on making improvements whenever and wherever opportunities arise. This won't happen in a skillful way unless the measurement system is supplying stability and capability data for analysis on a frequent basis. A process manager, as we described, has two improvement goals: 1) increase or decrease the center statistic (mean, median, or mode, whichever is more appropriate) depending on the direction of improvement, and 2) eliminate special cause variation and reduce or decrease common cause variation over time. Processes are notorious for not creating easy opportunities for improvement. Not always, but sometimes there are too many variables designed into a process for a process manager to be able to point to clearly identified problems and know exactly what the root cause or causes are so improvements can be made.

The commonly agreed upon approaches to process improvement include:

1. Standardize the process by developing a flowchart and process description and then make sure everyone who works in the process understands exactly what to do.

2. Stabilize the process by eliminating all special cause variation.

3. Make the process more capable by reducing common cause variation, including errors in the application of process steps.

4. Streamline the process by eliminating steps that don't add value, rerouting or reordering steps to make them more efficient, and reducing the amount of time between steps (Executive Learning Inc. 1995).

In process management language, standardizing the process (1) is done by carefully designing the process and then deploying it effectively. Stabilizing (2) and making the process more capable (3) require SPC data that we described in the measurement component of process management. A process manager uses control chart data to see if the process needs to be stabilized by looking for special causes of variation. Special causes of process variation are usually easy to identify because special causes are "special," they stick out like sore thumbs, they are unusual, and they are usually external to the process. Making a process capable is much more difficult than making it stable because common causes of variation are built into the process and difficult to identify. There are almost always more common causes of variation than there are special causes. Streamlining a process (4) is accomplished by having conversations with people who work in the process and listening to what they say about how the process actually functions, and contrasting those descriptions with the way the process was designed. People who work in processes usually have a wealth of ideas about how to streamline it. Another way to streamline a process is to benchmark it and apply what is learned from studying comparable exemplary processes.

Arthur (2007) suggests that if a process manager uses run or control charts, Pareto diagrams, and cause-and-effect diagrams (also called Ishikawa or fishbone diagrams) in that order, he or she would be able to identify and improve 90 percent of the causes of variation in a process. There are no empirical data to support his 90 percent claim, but it seems reasonable based on years of experience. Even if the actual number is closer to 70 or 80 percent, it is still a valuable suggestion to recommend using specific quality tools to simplify how a process manager approaches the task of improving processes. The last and most difficult 10 percent of process variation is improved by applying the ubiquitous plan–do–study–act (PDSA) improvement cycle or the more robust Six Sigma technology of define, measure, analyze, improve, and control (DMAIC). (We expand our discussion about these two improvement methodologies in the section titled Six Sigma.)

PROCESS MANAGEMENT QUESTIONS

The following are essential questions any process manager should be able to answer to show their management competency. These questions focus on the four key components of process management in a way that identifies and elaborates the basic purpose of each of the components. The questions would be appropriate to use in evaluating how well the process manager is fulfilling his or her responsibilities and obligations to the users or customers of the process, and their ability to achieve what the process is designed to produce. The implication here is that the person evaluating a process manager also has the prerequisite knowledge about processes and understands the statistical and technical nature of the questions to be able to judge the comprehensiveness of the process manager's answers.

1. *How do you clarify what the users' and customers' requirements or expectations are for the outcomes of the process you own?* (The answer, as we have described before, needs to distinguish between the different requirements and/or expectations of users, who will have specific requirements and expectations in terms of how the process works, and customers, who will have specific requirements and expectations in terms of the outcomes or results the process achieves.)

2. *Is the process that you manage producing stable or predictable amounts of variation each time it is used, without any special causes?* (Control chart data.)

3. *Is the process that you own capable, that is, is it able to meet or exceed customer requirements or expectations?* (Histogram data.)

4. *Where are the opportunities to make this process more stable and/or capable? Are opportunities for improvement found in a better process design, a better way to measure process results, or a more complete process deployment?* (So that the process is standardized across all who use the process.) *Are there opportunities to reduce process variation and/or to streamline the process by reducing the number of steps in the process?* (Flowchart assessment.)

5. *When was the last time you talked to the users and customers of this process to better understand how well they think the process is working and find out if they have any suggestions for improvement?* (This question is asked to reinforce the cultural value of continuous improvement and as a reminder that talking to the users and customers of the process is one of the most valuable sources of information about how the process is working that a process manager can find.)

6. *Who do you benchmark this process against? Are you satisfied that this is the best benchmark for this process? What have you learned from your benchmark(s) that has helped you improve this process?*

An Example Using the Six Questions

The following is an example of how a process manager who owns the curriculum development process might be expected to answer the six questions.

1. *How do you clarify what the users' and customers' requirements or expectations are for the outcomes of the process you own?* Each customer group is asked to identify what their requirements or expectations are for the curriculum process. These requirements come from the state department of education and district customers, parent and community customers, student customers, and teacher customers. The state and local customer requirements are identified using Web sites, publications, meetings, and person-to-person contact. Parent requirements are gathered using surveys, PTA meetings, and at other opportunities where parents are available. Community customer requirements come from survey information and district committees. Student requirements come from survey information and student focus groups led by principals. Teacher requirements are identified using surveys, focus groups, regular discussions with union leadership, and subject area curriculum committees. Sample sizes are calculated for each type of written survey because my goal is for survey results to be at a 95 percent confidence level with + or − 2 interval points. I achieved that goal with parents, students, and teachers but not with community members. In the future, I am going to identify community events that would allow me to collect survey information so I can accomplish the confidence and interval goals. (Page 25 identified a list of requirements for the curriculum development process.)

2. *Is the process you manage producing stable or predictable amounts of variation each time it is used without any special causes?* The major processes I own are curriculum development and teaching to standards. I have identified process targets based on customer requirements, translated those requirements into acceptable process variation, and then developed measures to monitor stability (see Figure 15). What I want to discuss with you this time is the progress we have made on our mathematics curriculum over the last year even though, as you can see, I have identified other measures for other parts of the process.

(See Appendix B for additional examples of a process management matrix.)

I operationally defined this measurement process so as to not introduce measurement variation, making sure we have an understanding about all aspects of the measurement process. I use operational definitions for all measurement activities (see Figure 16).

Before we discuss the results from the *np* chart (Figure 17), remember that having 10 percent or fewer of our students who do not meet mathematics standards is the same goal as having at least 90 percent of our mathematics students meet or exceed standards. When using the *np* chart, we need to use the number defective (does not meet) for the

Core quality processes	Process owner	Process target	Acceptable process variation	Process measure	Is the process stable? (Yes or no)	Is the process capable? (Yes or no)
Curriculum development	RE	100% improvement cycle compliance	No variation	Cycle time tracking chart		
		Subject area mean meets or exceeds the projected target	+ or – 1 standard deviation from target	Before and after implementation subject area test data *np* chart/histogram		
		90% stakeholder satisfaction with curriculum development process	+ or – 1 standard deviation from target	Satisfaction survey XmR chart		
Teaching to standards	RE	100% process compliance	All teachers score a 4 or 5 on the rubric scale	Teaching to the standard rubric XmR chart		

Figure 15   Process management matrix.

---

process target—90 percent of district students meet or exceed grade level mathematics standards.

measurement instrument(s)—*np* control chart using weekly district test data.

measurement process—Numbers of students that do not meet or exceed state and district standards are identified and grouped by the time the data were collected because that is how count or attribute data are measured using control charts. Count data uses the number/percent of students who do not meet the standard to calculate the chart. Sample test data for the past 3-year time period are used. The variable of the number/percent of students not meeting standards and the sequence of time (weekly) when the test data are gathered is entered into the QI Macros data sheet and an *np* control chart is graphed.

data analysis—The data are analyzed to determine if the mathematics instructional process is stable. Process stability is determined using the seven interpretation guidelines described in the QI Macros software. The goals are for the process to be stable, the mean or CL to be continuously improving, and for variation within the process to be decreasing. The analysis is used to immediately address special causes if they are detected. If the process displays predictable variation and the process is stable, then histogram data will be analyzed to confirm that the process is capable.

Figure 16   Operational definitions for measurement activities.

chart to work correctly. I don't use the term defective with my customers or colleagues for obvious reasons; calling students "defective" is not the best way to characterize this useful statistical quality tool. What this means is that when interpreting the chart, the vertical scale tells us that the better result is down—fewer students not meeting mathematics standards—and not up.

As you can see, the *np* control chart shows that from 2005 to 2007 the mean (CL) percentage of students who did not meet standards was 24. There is no number above the upper 3rd standard deviation, or upper control limit (UCL), and no number below

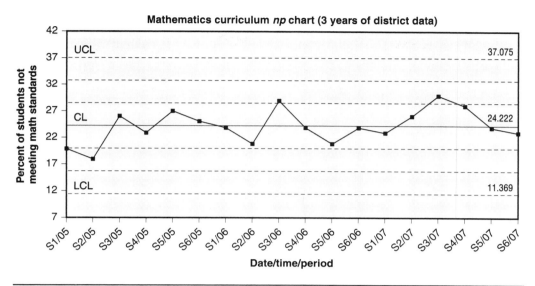

Figure 17   Three-year mathematics test data *np* chart.

the lower 3rd standard deviation, or lower control limit (LCL). In other words, there is no special cause variation in the mathematics curriculum. The process is stable. The tough problem for me as a process manager is to not confuse special causes of variation, which I treat in one way, with common cause variation, which I treat in another way. If I mix the two together, I won't be able to improve the process; in fact, I will make it much worse.

Standard deviation information helps us to understand processes because statisticians (specifically Shewhart [1939] but many others after him, including Deming [2000]) found that the common or normal variation in a process can be represented by + or − 3 standard deviations from the mean. Even though + or − 3 standard deviations is the norm, my customers, especially parents, thought that was too much variation and decided that + or −1 standard deviation is the most we want to tolerate when it comes to student achievement, so that is reflected in my variation targets. As you can see from the 3-year *np* chart, we have mostly stayed in that + or − 1 standard deviation range.

This was great news for me because I wouldn't have to identify and eliminate special causes first before I could do anything about the common variation in the mathematics curriculum process. From 2005 through 2007 all variation in the application of the mathematics curriculum was common cause variation, or the kind or variation we could predict from year to year with a great deal of certainty because it was inside the + or − 3 standard deviations range. The common variation of the mathematics curriculum means that for any testing period between 2005 through 2007, any result for a single test could be anywhere between the UCL (37 percent of students not meeting standards) to the LCL (11 percent of students not meeting standards). The total "not meeting standards" variation caused by the application of the mathematics curriculum is 26 (UCL − LCL). To have a mathematics curriculum with this much possible variation built into the application of the curriculum—although the actual variation is smaller—and with this percentage of students not meeting standards, was very upsetting to me—an intolerable situation. The histogram data, which we will talk about in a minute, confirmed this analysis.

3. *Is the process that you own capable, that is, is it able to meet or exceed customer requirements or expectations?* Figure 18 shows the operational definition I have drafted to answer this question.

Now I want to know if the mathematics curriculum is capable of achieving the 90 percent goal. I use histogram data (Figure 19) to confirm what I see in the *np* chart. I

---

process target—90 percent of district students meet or exceed grade level mathematics standards.

measurement instrument(s)—Histogram using *np* control chart data.

measurement process—The same data used to calculate the *np* chart are used to calculate the histogram. These numbers are entered into a QI Macros data sheet using the procedures for developing a histogram. Cells are formatted to the correct decimal precision. The upper and lower specification limits, the number of bars to display (usually a minimum of six), and C_p and C_{pk} are determined. The data are run to create a graph.

data analysis—The data are analyzed to determine if the mathematics curriculum process is capable of achieving the 90 percent target. Process capability is determined by analyzing the dispersion of students who meet or exceed standards in relation to the bell-shaped curve superimposed on the histogram. The C_p and C_{pk} numbers should be above 1.00 and the lower specification limit should be below 10 in order for the process to be declared capable. The goal is to verify that the process is capable and that the dispersion of student scores is normally distributed.

Figure 18   Operational definition for mathematics curriculum process.

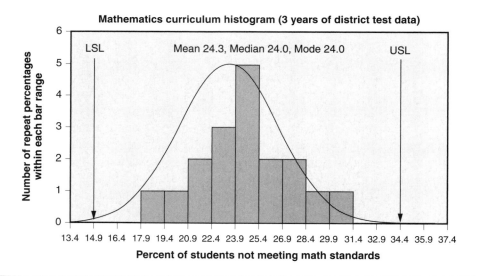

Figure 19   Three-year mathematics test data histogram.

want to know graphically how the data fall within a normal distribution, or a bell-shaped curve. This tells me if I'm dealing with data that are distributed normally or if those data are, for example, bimodal or skewed to the left or right. Having bimodal or skewed results will make the mean of the data much less important and it will create a much different discussion about what the data mean and why they are "shaped" this way.

To develop this histogram I used the 2005–07 data that created the *np* chart. I used QI Macros software because it also calculates the upper and lower specification limits to the process under study. In this case the upper specification limit (USL) was 33.5 and the lower specification limit (LSL) was 14.9. Remember that I said that from looking at the lower control limit number in the *np* chart (11), it didn't look like the mathematics curriculum was capable of achieving the 10 percent or fewer students not meeting standards. The 14.9 lower specification limit number tells me that was true. The lower and upper specification limits tell me that 99.73 percent of the time, a district mathematics test result will fall between 14.9 and 33.5 percent of students not meeting mathematics standards now and in the future, if nothing changes. That is what the mathematics curriculum was capable of achieving. The *np* chart and the histogram confirmed my diagnosis that the common cause variation built into the curriculum was excessive and that the curriculum, as currently applied, would not be able to deliver the quality of mathematics instruction necessary for us to achieve the 90 percent goal. The mathematics curriculum was stable (no special causes) but not capable of meeting our goal. We needed a drastic change.

4. *Where are the opportunities to make this process more stable and/or capable? Are opportunities for improvement found in a better process design, a better way to measure process results, or a more complete process deployment?* I brought the mathematics curriculum committee together in the winter of 2007 to redesign the mathematics curriculum and related instructional approaches. We reviewed the requirements from our curriculum customer groups to see how many of those requirements were being met by the current curriculum and which requirements would have to be addressed. The mathematics curriculum committee checked to see if there was a complete mathematics curriculum deployment. We calculated deployment to be at 98 percent. This told us that the variation in the process and the fact that it wasn't capable of achieving our 90 percent goal wasn't a deployment problem. Our district testing system had undergone validity and reliability studies the previous year by an outside contractor and the results were impressive. Not a measurement problem. Clearly a better curriculum design was indicated by the analysis of the *np* and histogram data. When all the variation within a process is common, the cause is the process. It is much more difficult to find causes of this variation because there are usually so many. When the mathematics curriculum committee used a cause-and-effect diagram, they found numerous causes under the major categories of teachers, instructional procedures, technology, materials, and students. We also knew that when there are many causes of variation, tinkering with the process will not achieve our goal. We felt that a totally new, innovative approach to redesigning the mathematics curriculum was needed, not simply small adjustments, so our improvement strategy was to benchmark sites that achieved exemplary mathematics results.

We benchmarked exemplary mathematics curricula, identifying those that create a 90 percent "meets or exceeds" rate, our stated student learning target. Lastly, we incorporated what we learned into a revised mathematics curriculum and piloted it that spring, including the use of a mathematics instructional flowchart. Deployment/implementation activities occurred over the summer and before school started.

Our two goals were to reduce the mean percent of students that were not meeting standards and to reduce the mathematics curriculum process variation. The 2008 data displayed on the *np* chart (Figure 20) show the result of the committee's work. The mean percentage of students not meeting standards (CL) dropped from 24 to 10. The common cause variation (difference between the UCL and the LCL) dropped from 26 to 18. The LCL between 2005 through 2007 was 11, giving us a suspicion that as designed, the mathematics curriculum could not achieve our 90 percent meets or exceeds standards goal. Clearly the 2008 LCL of 1.202 (meaning that it is possible for 98.708 percent of all mathematics students to meet standards on any given test) gives us a great deal of confidence that this goal can now be achieved. We will have to collect more data, because we need at least 8 to 9 data points to confirm a trend and we currently have only 6, but the dramatic improvement in results demonstrates that something significant happened. Our teachers share our initial enthusiasm about these changes. They see the difference these curriculum changes have made in the achievement and motivation levels of students every day.

5. *When was the last time you talked to the users and customers of this process to better understand how well they think the process is working and if they have any suggestions for improvement?* When the curriculum committee met, the first thing we did was to reaffirm the mathematics curriculum requirements by hosting customer focus groups.

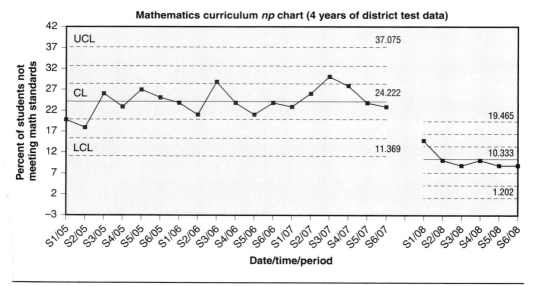

Figure 20   Four-year mathematics test data *np* chart.

6. *Who do you benchmark this process against? Are you satisfied that this is the best benchmark for this process? What have you learned from your benchmark(s) that has helped you improve this process?* The mathematics team decided on benchmarking as the method they thought would stimulate the innovative process as we redesigned the curriculum. The two ways we decided to find benchmark schools were to develop a scattergram of comparable school districts (Figure 21) across the metro area and to use the Just for the Kids opportunity gap bar charts (Figure 22) so we could broaden our search across the entire state. Because the data we needed are already on the state Department of Education Web site, we were able to apply the two benchmarking methods immediately and came up with the results we were looking for.

The scattergram (Figure 23) shows a slight (R^2 is .11) negative correlation between our district's mathematics curriculum and other comparable school districts, but that wasn't what was important. We were looking for outlier district mathematics programs. As you can see, the scattergram helped us find three districts in the lower right-hand part of the graph where only around 10 percent of their students but about 25 percent of our students were not exceeding standards. Their mathematics curriculum was achieving our goal.

The Just for the Kids Web site verified this data, so we did extensive benchmarking of those districts, including on-site visits and document review. We learned a great deal from them that was incorporated into the new curriculum.

---

process target—Identify exemplary practices.

measurement instrument—Scattergram.

measurement process—Comparable surrounding school districts are identified and mathematics performance data are gathered. District and subgroup performance averages in mathematics are used for comparisons. Scattergrams are developed by entering the data into a QI Macros data sheet.

data analysis—Data are analyzed to determine if the district is performing similarly to comparison school districts. Scattergrams are analyzed to determine if some comparison districts have results that would suggest that their programs should be benchmarked to learn what makes them work so well. Lessons learned by benchmarking are shared with appropriate committees, departments, and schools.

Figure 21   Operational definition for identifying exemplary practices.

---

process target—Identify exemplary practices.

measurement instrument(s)—Just for the Kids (opportunity gap bar charts).

measurement process—The iirc.niu.edu Web site is accessed as soon as the state date for the ISAT is posted each year. The JFTK opportunity gap bar charts are printed for each school and each grade level or subject area.

Data Analysis—The data are analyzed to determine if the mathematics instructional process performance meets or exceeds the top schools as compared with district achievement. The Top Comparable School chart is used to identify who these schools are. The analysis is used to benchmark those schools to determine what programs and practices are causing high student performance.

Figure 22   Operational definition for identifying exemplary practices.

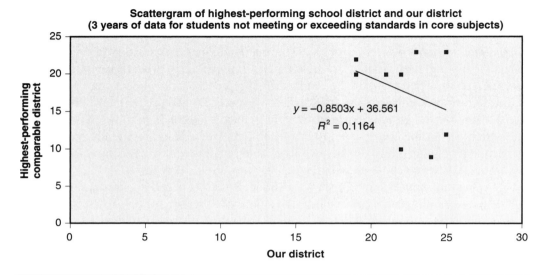

Scattergram of highest-performing school district and our district
(3 years of data for students not meeting or exceeding standards in core subjects)

$y = -0.8503x + 36.561$
$R^2 = 0.1164$

Figure 23 Benchmark scattergram.

The teachers on the mathematics curriculum committee found that the benchmarking process stimulated many great ideas that became part of the revised curriculum. The last act of the curriculum committee members was to develop the "should be" flowchart for the instructional part of the new curriculum.

THE TWO MAJOR QUALITY TOOLS THAT A PROCESS MANAGER MUST MASTER

This section provides additional information and examples of the two major tools we have already introduced that help process owners understand how to manage and improve processes: flowcharts and statistical process control (SPC). As we noted earlier, flowcharts and process maps are visual descriptions of each step in the process and how steps link together. A flowchart or process map graphically shows how the process should be applied to achieve the result the process was designed to produce. It is also used to analyze how to improve the process.

The second major tool necessary to understand process improvement is statistical process control (SPC). Statistical thinking is necessary to fully understand how processes are working. Statistical thinking answers the questions: Is the process stable or predictable? Is the process capable of achieving our goal? No mathematics is necessary for learning SPC measures. There are a number of software programs out there to do all the calculations accurately. (Note: The authors prefer the QI Macros software program because it has all the necessary SPC tools, is easy to use, and is inexpensive. It is a macro that attaches to Excel. It also has a decision tree to help the user decide which control chart would be the best fit for the data that have been collected.) The important knowledge a process manager has to master is how to choose the right control chart and how to analyze SPC data to make improvement decisions.

Flowcharting

When processes are designed, they should be flowcharted. In the third part of this book you will find a number of examples of flowcharted processes. A basic and absolutely essential skill for managers of processes is the ability to facilitate flowcharting a process, whether it is the development of a new design or the redesign of an old process. (Note: Almost any good quality tool book will have a description of how to facilitate the development of a flowchart. Those we have mentioned previously all have step-by-step descriptions of how to develop flowcharts.)

For example, think of yourself as the process manager for curriculum development. You might bring together a team of teachers, principals, central office staff, and maybe an outside expert in curriculum development—what would be called a cross-functional process mapping team. Cross-functional means that there are team members who function in or work on different aspects of curriculum and have different experiences with and perspectives about the curriculum development process. The team would make a decision about what to include in the flowcharting activities. Will the flowchart include not only the curriculum development process itself, but the pilot or field-testing process and the deployment or implementation process also? A clear definition of what the flowcharting process will include, where it will start and where it will finish, is an absolute necessity before the cross-functional team work begins.

Flowcharting or process mapping would begin with the development of an "as is" map of the curriculum development process currently in use in the district. (Note: This assumes that a flowchart of the curriculum development process does not exist. If it does, then that is used as the "as is" chart or map. The team then checks the existing flowchart for accuracy.) The "as is" flowchart is developed based on the descriptions of team members as they talk about the specific activities that happen during curriculum development, as well as important decision points for a variety of curriculum development projects that are currently being developed or just recently completed. The team begins the flowcharting process by dividing the curriculum development process into its major components. Each component has descriptions of the activities that take place during that part of the process. It might look something like Figure 24.

The cross-functional team then begins to map out a specific flowchart for each of the four curriculum development components using standard flowchart symbols. The level of detail is up to the team members but it should account for all major decisions in the activities of the component. The "as is" flowchart should also identify the time of completion for important chunks or activities of each curriculum development process component as well as for the whole process. Concerns about or problems with the current curriculum development process are recorded throughout the development of the "as is" flowchart. As the last "as is" activity, each individual component flowchart is merged with the next to create one complete flowchart of the curriculum development process.

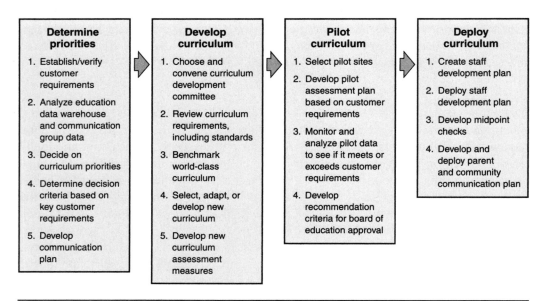

Figure 24 Flowchart of major components of curriculum development process.

Upon completion of the "as is" flowchart, the process manager might have members of the mapping team take the map back to their individual schools or departments for review and critique. It is amazing how useful it is to have other critical friends look at the flowchart and ask questions or make suggestions. This always helps to clarify the work of the mapping team and leads to further clarifications and a more realistic "as is" flowchart.

After a few weeks, the mapping team would get back together to make final adjustments to the "as is" flowchart and to record any additional concerns or problems about the process as it is currently practiced. The mapping team then begins the construction of the "should be" flowchart to address all the concerns recorded by team members and district-critical friends. The "should be" flowchart is characterized by the following important guidelines:

- A definitive beginning and ending point for the curriculum development process is determined.

- A strict adherence to all identified customer requirements.

- Reduction in cycle time between the beginning and ending points by streamlining activities within the process.

- Identification of specific action items that would help to systematize and reduce cycle times.

- Show specifically where concerns recorded by team members and critical friends have been addressed in the "should be" flowchart.

After the development of the "should be" flowchart, the process manager would put together a document that is divided into sections that correspond to the specific actions and decision points identified in the "should be" flowchart. Each section begins with a detailed elaboration of either a curriculum development action or decision. The stakeholders involved in the action or decision are identified, and the role they play in the action or decision is described. Each section also includes any checklists, memos, or forms that need to be completed or maintained as part of the action or decision. The cycle time recording sheet (Figure 25) is an example of what might be included in documenting the curriculum development process.

A third thing process managers must focus on is the need to make processes efficient. This is partially measured by process cycle time, or the time from when something enters the process to the time it leaves the process, or from the time it enters a step in the process to the time it leaves that step. Using our curriculum development example, a cycle time tracking chart might look something like Figure 25.

A bus route has a cycle time. Submitting an invoice, accounts receivable, serving hot lunch, facilities maintenance, a central stores materials order, book checkout, budgeting, teaching a concept or concept mastery, professional growth activities, special education identification, book adoptions, technology help desk requests, are all examples of processes that have cycle times. Once desired versus actual cycle time has been measured, improving efficiency is usually addressed by analyzing the steps designed into a process because the fewer the steps that create the same result, the more efficient the process. A flowchart analysis would be required to see if unnecessary steps exist that cause wasted time or if there is a duplication of steps that also causes the process to take more time and effort than is needed. The time when a process moves from one department or building to another is also a place to look for a way to streamline the process. The other tool besides a flowchart that a process manager should use to identify inefficiencies in the process is the SIPOC quality tool we introduced earlier in this book, on page 11.

Statistical Process Control (SPC)

A control chart is nothing more than a run chart on statistical steroids, and the only statistics you have to concern yourself with are means and standard deviations. A control chart gives you a graphic picture about how well a process performs over time. The human mind does not do a very good job of analyzing numerical data, especially in table form; it can do a much better job of analysis when given a picture of the numbers in an organized way. Control charts give a visual representation of the numbers that represent the functioning of a very abstract and complicated thing, a process. Control chart data also move people away from using common sense to analyze data—a notoriously poor way to try and understand the behavior of processes and systems—to a much more precise and accurate statistical sense of data interpretation.

A basic purpose of a control chart is to track improvements to a process over time to see if there is actual improvement or if what looks like improvement is just random variation in the process. To review, control charts minimize the chances of making two

Cycle time monitor: _____

Curriculum development action or decision	District 15 group(s) responsible	Predicted completion time	Initiation date	Actual completion time
Recommendation for curriculum development	Department of instruction			
Cabinet approval for curriculum development	Cabinet			
Board of education approval for curriculum development	Board of education			
Convene the curriculum development team	Department of instruction			
Seek/find or develop a curriculum	Department of instruction			
Pilot curriculum	Department of instruction			
Conduct focus group meetings	Department of instruction			
Prepare recommendation for curriculum adoption	Curriculum development team			
Curriculum adoption recommendation taken to the board of education for approval	Board of education			
Staff development for adopted curriculum	Department of instruction			
Evaluation of results and determination of whether requirements are met	Department of instruction			
Process evaluation	Department of instruction/curriculum development team			
Time totals				

Figure 25   Cycle time recording sheet.

kinds of mistakes: 1) acting as though something out of the ordinary happened (for example, claiming something improved or got worse) when nothing really did, and 2) failing to act when something out of the ordinary really happened. For example, when test score data are reported in newspapers there are often claims of significant improvement when those improvements are only the common cause variation within the subject area being tested. In other words, districts and schools take credit for improving student achievement when there was no actual improvement, just normal variation in the process occurring from year to year (or whatever the time interval is between tests). A few years back, a statistician took a school district to task for making academic improvement claims to the public that weren't true, especially when those statements were being used to support a bond election. All he needed was a background in control chart and histogram application and analysis and a basic understanding of processes to cause a good deal of embarrassment to the leadership of that district. Likewise, after test score reports come out in local newspapers there are sometimes stories about how a school or school district is falling apart based on one set of poor test scores when those results could have been influenced by a special cause. Special causes are not excuses, but they will occur periodically and they need to be explained appropriately to customer groups. Overreacting after having just experienced a special cause is not leadership but a thoughtless reaction that creates confusion and wastes time and energy. Unfortunately, this happens all too often and wastes way too many resources. Yes, a special cause needs to be found, and plans need to be made so it doesn't happen again, but that is a much different response than acting in desperation to fix a special cause as though it were a common cause. It is one of the best examples of poor leadership in school districts today.

Control chart data help a process owner do the following:

- Understand how much variation is built into a process

- Monitor the results of a process over time

- See the effects of a change to a process over time

- Provide a more accurate basis for predicting how well a process will perform in the future

We have focused our attention on making the distinction between common and special cause variation using single instances of a number appearing outside either the UCL or the LCL. There exist other rules to help the analyst look at a string of numbers (usually 8 or 9) in a run or control chart that also may be signaling a situation where a special cause might exist. The rule makers don't disagree on significant issues in interpreting the data, but there are subtle differences in a number of instances, usually based on theoretical assumptions found in the application of statistics. We have not found these rule differences to be a problem, and most statistical software will let you choose which set of rules you want to apply to the data being analyzed. Following are examples of some of these rules, developed in this case by Wheeler (2003), to give you a sense of how much information gets overlooked or not analyzed correctly because of a lack of knowledge related to rule interpretation. (Note: Wheeler's use of the word "assignable" is the same as our use of the word "special.")

There are five detection rules for interpreting control charts (and in certain instances, run charts):

1. *Detection rule one: points outside the limits.* A single point outside the computed limits (UCL or LCL) should be taken as a signal of the presence of an *assignable* (special) cause that has a *dominant* effect.

2. *Detection rule two: runs about the central line.* Eight successive values on the same side of the central line (mean) will be taken as an indication of the presence of an *assignable* (special) cause that has a *weak* but *sustained* effect.

3. *Detection rule three: runs near the limits.* Three out of four successive values in the upper 25%, or three out of four successive values in the lower 25%, of the region between the limits may be taken as a signal of the presence of an *assignable* (special) cause that has a *moderate* but *sustained* effect.

4. *Detection rule four: runs beyond two sigma.* When two out of three successive values fall more than two sigma above the central line or more than two sigma below the central line, they may be interpreted as a signal of the presence of an *assignable* (special) cause that has a *moderate* but *sustained* effect.

5. *Detection rule five: runs beyond one sigma.* When four out of five successive values fall more than one sigma above the central line, or more than one sigma below the central line, they may be interpreted as a signal of the presence of an *assignable* (special) cause that has a *moderate* but *sustained* effect.

FLOWCHARTING PROCESS IMPROVEMENT

Practicing what we preach seems to be a reasonable approach to summarizing how processes are improved. The flowchart assumes that a process has been designed, measured, and deployed. After deployment the process manager will want to use this flowchart to continue to make the process meet or exceed the requirements and expectations of customer groups. Using the Figure 26 flowchart, a step-by-step description of process improvement goes as follows.

The process manager needs to know what the process is required to achieve. An example of a process requirement is that 90 percent of all students need to meet or exceed state standards in reading and mathematics. Another example is that 98 percent of buses deliver students to their schools on time. If the process does not have requirements, you don't have processes; you have happenings or activities without a purpose. Sources used to identify process requirements or expectations include agencies that set standards or customers that use the process. Clear target statements of process requirements are a necessary first step in process improvement.

Next, the process manager needs to know if the process is stable or predictable. The way to improve a process differs depending on whether or not it is stable. The stability of a process is determined by running a process measure called a control chart. If the process is unstable, that means there are special causes of process variation showing up in the control chart data that must be identified and resolved. A process needs to be stable or predictable before you can go to the next step of determining capability.

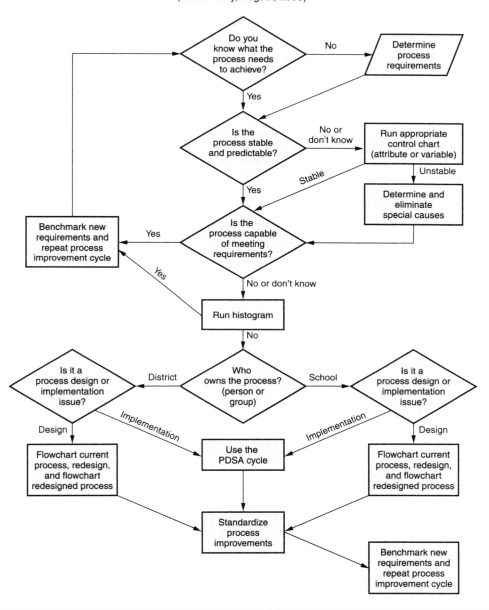

Figure 26 Process improvement flowchart.

Once all special causes have been resolved and the process is stable, the process manager needs to find out if it is capable. Capability means that the process is adequately designed to meet or exceed the 90 percent student achievement requirement or the 98 percent on-time requirement examples mentioned above. If teachers are working to meet or exceed the 90 percent achievement target but are required to use district curriculum and instructional processes that are incapable of meeting that target, then you have put teachers in the position of having to achieve the impossible. Measuring capability is an extremely important calculation because it tests the assumptions of the designers about what they think the process is capable of achieving. You can not determine capability by looking just at means or averages. The measurement of capability is usually done with histograms that calculate upper and lower specification limits and C_{pk} to determine what the process is capable of achieving in relation to what you want it to achieve (Abbott 1999). (Note: We have not introduced the metric of C_{pk} because it is fairly technical. C_{pk} is a metric that indicates whether a process is capable or not and is calculated automatically by the software we use to develop histograms. All the sources we have recommended to develop a better understanding of SPC also explain C_{pk}.)

If the process manager knows the process is stable and capable, then it is time to benchmark new process requirements or make the process more efficient. If the process is stable and predictable but not capable, then that information is used to decide if improvements should be focused on redesigning the process or on the implementation of the process. If the histogram mean, LSL, and/or USL show that the process is clearly not capable of achieving requirements like the 90 percent student achievement target, then the process manager would know that a redesign of the process is necessary. That would prompt the person or persons responsible for the process to flowchart the current process and then redesign the flowchart by incorporating improvements into the design of the process that would have the greatest possible chance of closing the performance gap. If the process is capable but there is unacceptable variation above and below the mean, especially if the variation is between departments, schools, or classrooms, then the focus of improvement would more likely be on better deployment or implementation of the process.

Once the new design has been flowcharted or deployment activities have been strengthened, the process manager would devote his or her time to standardizing improvements, making sure the steps in the flowchart are understood and being followed or that deployment is occurring as intended.

Lastly, assuming everything happens as planned, and what was planned addressed the right issues, the process manager will always be looking for other ways to continue to improve the process. This usually involves benchmarking other similar processes to find exemplary practices that might add more effectiveness and efficiency to the process that he or she owns.

To review, we have stated that to manage processes requires skill and expertise in two areas. One is to be able to visualize a process, usually in the form of a flowchart or process map. The other is to be able to monitor the process to see if it is behaving in a stable and capable manner using control charts and histograms.

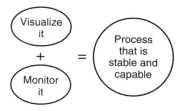

Figure 27   Process management formula.

SIX SIGMA

This section of the book is intended to be a forceful argument for the use of statistically advanced quality tools by process managers. We assert that the typical quality tools used by process managers, usually in a plan–do–study–act (PDSA) framework, are not adequate to address significant and difficult process improvements.

Let's begin this discussion about Six Sigma with a short quiz. Please answer the following questions:

1. What process improvement methodology has become the most popular in the world today but is almost unknown to leaders in education?

2. What process improvement methodology is currently creating results that have not been paralleled by any other quality methodology?

3. What process improvement methodology was first applied to the field of manufacturing and has since found considerable acceptance and success in the area of healthcare and the service sector but not in education?

4. What process improvement methodology requires leaders, managers, and teams to learn new statistical and quality tools that not only will improve process performance but also help staff gain greater acceptance of solutions that create performance excellence?

5. What popular process improvement methodology would expose the inefficiency and ineffectiveness of those who have developed a high tolerance for inefficiency and ineffectiveness and create endless excuses about why it won't work in "our" organization or in the field of education?

If you are at all attuned to context clues, the answers to this test are a no-brainer. Six Sigma is a process improvement methodology used by process managers to create breakthrough improvements. It is a five-step process that applies sufficiently powerful quality tools at each step so that an in-depth understanding of the causes of variation is applied to develop solutions that are equal to the problem at hand.

We introduced a premise by Arthur (2007) earlier in the book, stating that 90 percent of variation causes in processes could be reduced or eliminated by using the quality tools of run or control charts, Pareto diagrams, and cause-and-effect diagrams. Run or control charts identify the problem, Pareto charts dissect the problem, and cause-and-effect diagrams identify where improvements can be made. We cautioned that there isn't any good, quantifiable data to support this claim, but there is an accumulation of practical experience that agrees with the underlying premise that the application of some fairly simple quality tools can solve the greatest majority of process problems. This is the idea of picking the "low hanging fruit" applied to process management. The bad news is that the remaining 10 percent or so of process problems are difficult to identify and solve, are usually mission-critical, and require a sophisticated framework applying statistical quality tools if these process problems are ever to be adequately addressed. Being able to solve the most difficult process problems is, as they say, why a process manager makes the big bucks.

PDSA is a framework, and a very good one, for managing change and process improvement. PDSA has been enthusiastically embraced by those in education as a useful problem-solving and change management process. Based on our observations, PDSA's greatest virtue is its simplicity. Four logical and reasonable steps can get the problem solver from problem identification to solution fairly painlessly and without too much stress. PDSA works, but not as effectively as it needs to, especially given the fact that the improvement of learning for all students is our goal. There are a few Baldrige award–winning school districts (Iredell–Statesville, Jenks, District 15, Pearl River) that have optimized the application of PDSA and have impressive improvements to show for their efforts. They have taken the PDSA methodology about as far as it can go and would probably find that the DMAIC framework provides the methodology that could carry these school districts to new levels of achievement.

The quality tools used in PDSA are simple if you think of quality tools on a continuum from simple to complex. Whether they are simple or complex, of course, depends on the skill mastery of the process manager in correctly applying and facilitating the use of quality tools. As an aside, as significant as this is, it is rare to find process managers that are evaluated in part on their quality tool knowledge and facilitation ability, which is another example of organizational misalignment (specifically, the misalignment between necessary job competencies and the evaluation of those competencies).

In their book *Six Sigma,* Harry and Schroeder (2000) make a statement that adds perspective to the issue we are addressing. They say:

> Statistics allow us to measure, improve, and monitor the processes within our organizations. Statistics are the tool that separates common sense reasoning from extraordinary reasoning.

This statement should shake your PDSA comfort zone. It makes clear the need to rethink how processes are measured but also that what you measure needs a level of statistical analysis that creates extraordinary reasoning. PDSA seems a very capable change management framework for incremental improvements but falls short when it comes to creating breakthrough or extraordinary solutions to education's most perplexing problems. That may be one of the reasons they are still around. Part of the failure of PDSA to create extraordinary gains is that the statistical tools used in most PDSA applications are simply not up to the task. Six Sigma is an improvement on PDSA, not something totally new. It redefines the steps and uses different tools for each step. Even though this is a refinement of the PDSA process, it results in considerable improvements in how well processes function and the results they produce.

Six Sigma is an outrageous concept. It asserts that the goal is to make process variation so small that only 3.4 defects will show up in one million parts. For example, if you had a process to make a bolt with precise requirements or specifications (tolerances), you would achieve a six sigma level if after making 1,000,000 bolts only 3.4 were rejected because they did not meet requirements. You actually experience a process that creates a better outcome than six sigma when you board an airplane. The domestic airline fatality rate is 0.52 people per million who fly. Comparing three sigma to six sigma results means that at three sigma 2000 articles of mail are lost each hour and at six sigma one article of mail is lost each hour. Fifteen minutes of unsafe drinking water occur each day at a three sigma level, and three minutes of unsafe drinking water occur each year at a six sigma level (Arthur 2007). Six sigma results are very real and necessary for our safety and well-being.

You would say that producing learners is very different than making bolts, and you would be absolutely right for so many obvious reasons. Most educational processes that have been measured produce results that are between two (69.1 percent) and three (93.3 percent) sigma, so the concept of achieving six sigma has no practical reality. But the concept of moving educational outcomes from a two to a three sigma and from a three to a four sigma (99 percent) makes a great deal of sense. The issue is that you will look long and hard to find any examples of PDSA methodology creating a six sigma result, but there are many examples of DMAIC (the Six Sigma methodology is called DMAIC, for define, measure, analyze, improve, and control) creating that result. Here are some reasons why:

1. The *plan* step in PDSA does a reasonable job in describing what the problem or issue is that needs to be addressed and improved. The tool used is usually some kind of prioritization process like a Pareto diagram to sort out the less significant many and isolate the few problems or issues that would seem to create the biggest payoff to the organization and its customers, especially students. The *define* step in DMAIC, on the other hand, pushes the intent of this step by validating the benefits or impact of this improvement priority to the organization and then by creating or validating a flowchart of the process to be improved, following what we know about good process management. A SIPOC diagram is also created so that the full implication of system interaction with the process is understood. The define step produces a much deeper analysis of the problem that better informs all following steps in the improvement process than is typically seen in the plan step.

2. There is no comparable step in PDSA to the *measure* step in DMAIC. This step is where determination of the stability and capability of the process under examination takes place. Inputs and outputs of the process are carefully identified and measured so that variables that contribute to the problem are identified and their contribution is given some sort of value. The measurement system itself is scrutinized to make sure it is not

contributing to the problem. The result is a set of validated data from multiple perspectives that create a rich description of the problem and its causes. Based on our many experiences with PDSA, we have yet to see something similar to the measure step occur in the plan step.

3. The *analyze* step in DMAIC would still be a part of the *plan* step of PDSA. Although improvement teams are getting better at this, there is still a maddening tendency when using PDSA for them to go from identifying the problem to finding a solution without first looking for root cause. Any improvement process that does not identify root cause is a wasted effort. Without finding root cause the team might as well do what we described in the beginning of the book and find an administrator, ask him or her what conference they have just attended and what program or practice impressed them, and try it. Throwing darts at solutions tacked to a wall would work just as well. Implementing something without careful analysis of the problem signifies a lack of competency on the part of the improvement team facilitator. Because SPC statistical tools are not used in PDSA, conversations about causes of process variation and process stability and capability do not happen. This is a significant deficit that leads to shallow analysis of the problem and identification of root cause. Think for a moment about an improvement team that mistakes a special cause for a common cause and spends their time developing improvement strategies for the wrong reasons.

4. The *do* step in PDSA is the same as the *improve* step in DMAIC. The difference is that usually in the improve step, one of the first things the improvement team will do is create a "should be," or redesigned, flowchart so that the improvement is graphically displayed and understood by those who are putting the solution into practice. The DMAIC improve step treats this activity as an "experiment" that may succeed or fail, which means that this step is carefully controlled in the usual manner of a scientific experiment. When PDSA teams plan for the do step, it often seems a foregone conclusion that the solution will succeed, and this leads to a lack of rigor as the solution is being implemented. The DMAIC improve step also includes the PDSA *study* step.

5. The last step in DMAIC, *control,* is similar to the *act* step in PDSA except that it focuses much more on standardizing the improvements that have produced the gains that were anticipated. This includes using the metrics and control charts, making any final corrections to the flowchart, developing appropriate documentation, and aligning policies and practices to the new improvements. Although the act step in PDSA is designed to create a successful end to the improvement cycle, in practice there is not the same kind of attention paid to this step as what is required for the control step in DMAIC.

We have developed PDSA and DMAIC linear flowcharts (Figures 28 and 29) to show the differences in the two improvement methodologies and illustrate the appropriate quality tools used during each step.

Even though DMAIC uses five steps instead of the four in PDSA, we think you can see how closely the four PDSA steps match up to the five in DMAIC. You can think of DMAIC as an evolutionary improvement of PDSA. It is the suggested quality tools related to each step and the way the steps have been sequenced that make the DMAIC

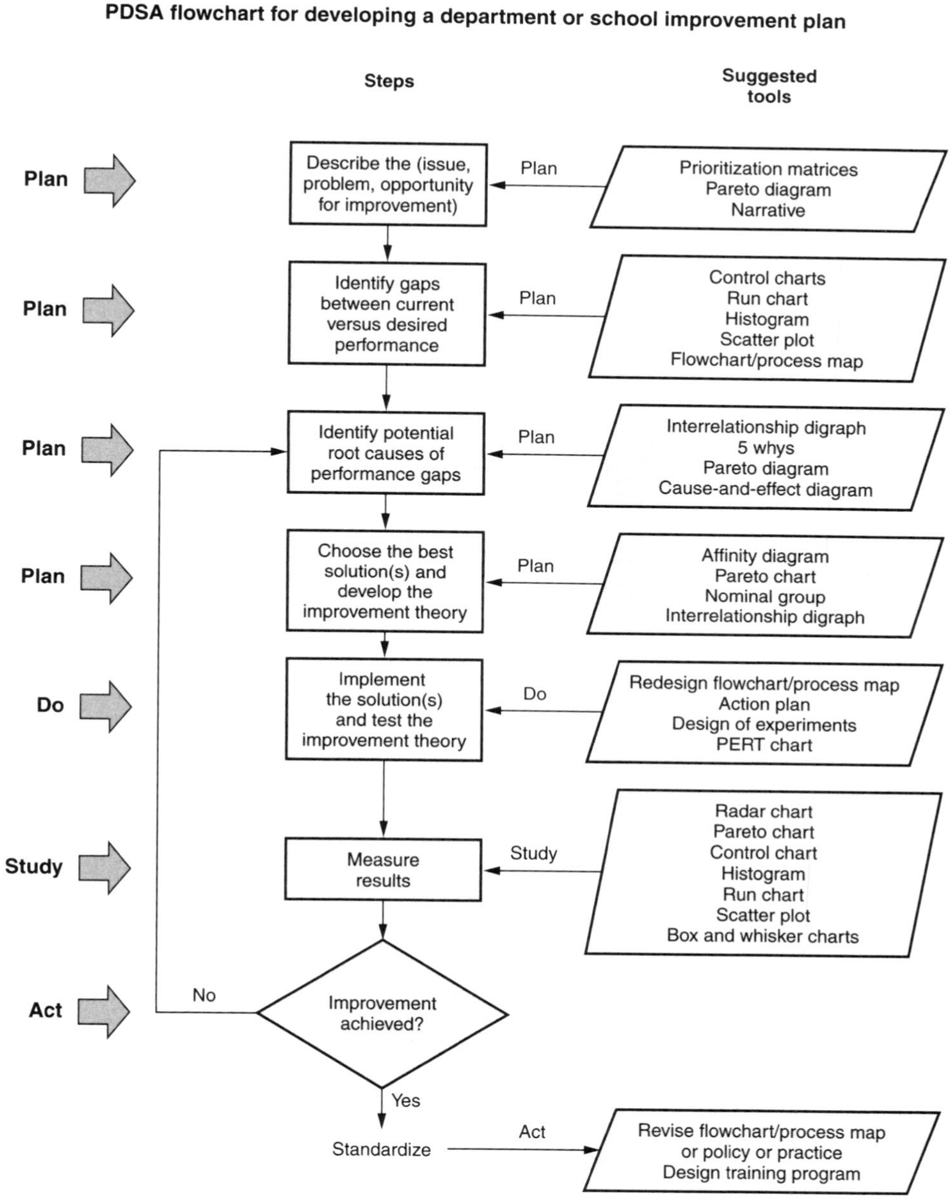

PDSA flowchart for developing a department or school improvement plan

Figure 28 PDSA flowchart.

improvement process so much more powerful. The tools are found on the more complex side of the quality tool continuum and require more statistical skill. They are not that much more difficult because you have already learned the basics of control charts and histograms, for example.

Can you use DMAIC tools with PDSA? Yes you can, but the fit will not be as natural. Each step in DMAIC is much more focused and robust than those in PDSA.

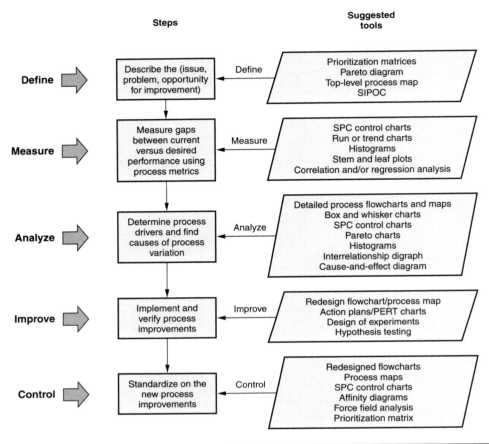

DMAIC for developing a department or school improvement plan

Figure 29   DMAIC flowchart.

DMAIC simply creates better process improvements than the way PDSA is currently being applied. We are not suggesting using Six Sigma methodology to create six sigma results in education, but we are saying that Six Sigma methodology will create much better results than those we are currently getting from PDSA.

It is highly recommended that process managers be trained in DMAIC so they can bring that expertise to the improvement of processes. The American Society for Quality (ASQ) provides levels of training in Six Sigma (White, Yellow, Green, and Black Belts) so a process manager can ease into this new process improvement methodology. In fact, having a PDSA background makes the transition much easier. For most process problems, PDSA will work quite well; but for other especially difficult process improvement issues, DMAIC is the obvious choice.

DMAIC is a more mature methodology than PDSA. It has undergone extensive development and review in some of the most challenging environments and created exceptional process improvements. It is the new standard for process improvement, bringing a necessary end to commonsense thinking and ushering in a new era of statistical reasoning that creates extraordinary results. (Note: This new era of DMAIC is actually about 20 years old and has stood the test of time. It is a well-validated approach to process improvement.) When it comes to creating the best possible education for all students, do you want to use *good* process improvement tools and methodology or *extraordinary* tools and methodology to make that happen?

CONCLUSION: PROCESSES ARE VITAL COMPONENTS OF SYSTEMS

"Feedback is your friend" is an important belief for everyone in a school district to hold and to act on. Likewise, "variation is the enemy" is a belief that every employee in a school district should understand and, more importantly, should be actively engaged in eliminating. This is one organizational enemy that should be shown no mercy, for its victims are the students the district has said it will educate. When we see a student fail, we know that the real failure is the process that was supposed to make that student a success. Failing students are the symptoms of failing processes, and failing processes are the result of people that have neither the skills nor knowledge to be a competent process manager.

In much the same way that we create the expectation that all teachers are teachers of reading, we should create the expectation that all district employees are process managers. Everyone in a school district has a title like teacher, superintendent, principal, support staff, board member, or director that describes what role that person plays in the school district. It doesn't matter what their job title says, the real title all district employees should hold is process manager. This is why all job descriptions and evaluations need to be closely aligned to the skills and competencies for process managers that we have outlined in this book.

Implied in this title shift is the necessity of having the knowledge and skills to be able to artfully manage the four components (design, measurement, deployment, and improvement) of process management. We understand that this is not easy, but it is doable. You are well on your way after having read this book. Additional training is needed in SPC and/or Six Sigma to develop statistical expertise and expand the application and mastery of more sophisticated quality tools. As we mentioned earlier in the book, many businesses already have this expertise and might become a coach or tutor to your school district. ASQ has excellent training programs that address all the knowledge and skill areas found in this book. If we ruled the educational world, every administrator would have a quality tool reference on their desk such as *The Quality Toolbox*, Second Edition, by Nancy Tague (2005) that provides the necessary background of a tool so that the person using it understands its intent and application. This example also references the more difficult to understand statistical tools we have been describing so that the practitioner can apply those tools appropriately.

We recommend getting software to do all the SPC calculations. There are many elegant programs available. Besides QI Macros, which we have mentioned, we use

CHARTrunner by PQ Systems. This statistical software package is very powerful and can do the appropriate calculations using data from multiple sources, which is especially useful for those school districts that need to export data from existing data warehouses. There are other software programs available, and we recommend a thorough analysis before purchase.

One thing that the school district can do immediately is to flowchart processes. This single activity could do more to advance process improvements than anything else. Even though this might strike fear in the hearts of administrators, we strongly recommend taking on the task of developing an instructional flowchart such as the examples in Part Three. Nothing could have a more long-term benefit than having a districtwide discussion about what instruction should look like. We can tell you the first reaction will be that a flowchart inhibits teacher creativity. That couldn't be farther from the truth. There is nothing that stops a teacher's creativity within the flowchart framework. What this flowchart does address is the "anything goes" thinking about teaching when a critical mass of research shows how best practice is applied. Having different flowcharts for teaching different grades, subjects, and students would be a great way to foster innovation and to test the models to see if they produce different results. We find these flowcharts very dynamic in that teachers are constantly improving them over time, refining exactly what should happen. This is a big risk/big payoff kind of activity.

The services that central office departments and school staff provide to district and school stakeholders are too important to be left solely to the good intentions of very competent people. A mixture of those good intentions with the application of selected quality tools to design, measure, deploy, or improve processes is needed in order to move the district to a new level of achievement excellence. Without understanding how processes behave, improvement becomes at best a guessing game. There is no focus, no ability to identify causes and select the right strategies, and no ability to improve a process except to do what Edison did when inventing the light bulb, which was to try many possible solutions before the right one was found. No organization has the time, resources, expendable staff motivation or expertise, or stakeholder patience to be an Edison. With a proper understanding and application of quality tools, that doesn't have to happen. Department and school leaders work on the system and processes within the system to improve them, with the absolutely essential help of the professional and support staff.

One additional resource that should be explored is the North Star Project supported by the American Productivity and Quality Center (APQC). As Grayson states, and as we have emphasized throughout this book, "Outcomes are created by processes, and if you do not improve the processes that generate the outcomes, you can't improve outcomes" (Grayson, 2009).

Now that you know all this, when can we expect to read about the exemplary improvements your district has achieved? Education needs more examples of extraordinary performance, and we think you are the perfect candidate. We wish you the best!

Part Three
Process Examples

The question is often asked, "How do you move an entire school system to operate differently?" The answer to this question is that you define and deploy the processes that you want everyone in the district to use. While it may sound like a very simple solution to a very imposing challenge, process really is at the heart of school improvement. What may sound simple, but in reality is very difficult, is to define processes in a school district.

We have traditionally used two major strategies in operating school districts. The first is defining administrative procedures and the second is collaboration around professional judgment. When you look at most school districts' administrative procedures, they define the behavior of individuals within the district. The procedures say what can and can not be done. They may also define the sequence of events or actions that should be taken. However, they almost never define the desired results and assess whether or not the results are obtained. They are used with a compliance mentality to determine if the right actions were taken in the right order, given a specific situation.

Collaboration around professional judgment is an important tool to use to resolve issues or address problems and develop buy-in on the part of the participants. This strategy works when the participants ensure that there is an effort to look at best practices and not just collaborate around people's collective opinions. When involving people in decision making, it is critical that consideration is given to the research, information, or data that demonstrates the best method to achieve the desired results. It is not effective, and sometimes quite harmful, to have a collaborative decision that does not address the real issue or problem.

Defining and deploying processes within an organization are strategies that overcome the shortfalls of the methods described above. If a school district can effectively define the process needed to teach children a desired outcome and then deploy the process so that all employees in the organization use it, the district will achieve the results it desires. Community Consolidated School District 93 began this type of effort in 2006 by deciding to define its processes rather than to update its administrative procedures manual. Figures 30 through 35 are results of those efforts. Many different processes have been defined and deployed within the organization. Efforts are ongoing to continue to develop quality processes for critical functions in the district and to improve the processes that are already in place. The district uses a quality process template to define every process in place. The template remains the same so that there is a common understanding among employees as to how to use process documents. Each process that is defined includes the following components:

Front page:

- A narrative description of the process and what it is intended to accomplish
- The connections between the process and the district's mission statement
- The definition of which stakeholders are involved in the process and how they are involved
- The improvement cycle that is used to improve the process

Back page:

- A flowchart of the process

Inside pages:

- Examples of relevant documents and tools associated with the process

This common format enables employees to develop and use processes in a timely manner. It ensures that all the information necessary for an employee to understand a process is located in one place. The definition of quality processes within the district also permits stakeholders who are not regular users of a process to understand the process when the need arises. All District 93 processes are currently collected in one location within the schools and online so that all employees have ready access to the information.

The effort to define quality processes began slowly with a few employees trying to define their most critical and frequent processes. These initial efforts began with administrators, but the initiative has grown into a far more common practice among employees. It is now common to hear staff members say, "We need a quality process" for an issue when they are working on improvement efforts.

Another critical component of the successful use of processes is professional development. While it is critical to have processes defined, it is also important to have the processes deployed through staff development and usage efforts. Initial training through staff development activities can provide a starting point for use. However, it is critical that once a process is developed, the process owner monitors its implementation by assessing how widely and appropriately it is being used throughout the organization. Having the best process in the world but not using it comprehensively is no better than having everyone use an ineffective process. The results in both cases will be poor and a waste of time and energy.

Community Consolidated School District 93 has defined 50-plus processes. The staff continues to define new processes and improve developed processes because the district firmly believes that process improvement is at the heart of systematic change within the organization.

CCSD93

Working together, nurturing the potential

Quality Process

K-2 Literacy Intervention Programs

The K-2 Literacy Intervention Programs provide intensive support in reading to identify students at the kindergarten through second grade levels. Three programs have been designed to support our primary students: All Aboard (kindergarten), Bright Start (first grade), and Blast Off (second grade). All programs are structured to supplement classroom reading and writing instruction and are aligned to Illinois Standards as well as the National Reading Panel report issued in 2000 identifying the following key skills and methods central to reading achievement: phonemic awareness, phonics, fluency, vocabulary, and text comprehension.

Our Curriculum Coordinator collaborates with the Reading Specialists to implement and monitor the programs. Twenty K-2 Literacy Staff members are trained in assessment and instructional procedures. Training is provided by the Curriculum Coordinator and Reading Specialists on an ongoing basis throughout the year.

All Aboard: This program is offered to qualifying kindergarten students second semester. Instruction is provided in an individual tutorial setting for fifteen minutes each day. Each highly structured, intensive and interactive lesson focuses on building and strengthening the following skills: alphabet recognition, letter sounds, letter production, phonetic awareness, concept of word, sight vocabulary, beginning writings and book reading.

Bright Start: This program is offered to qualifying first-grade students first and second semester. Instruction is provided to groups of two students for twenty-five minutes each day. Each highly structured, intensive, and interactive lesson focuses on building and strengthening the following skills: letter sounds, word concept, word recognition, phonemic awareness, decoding, reading fluency, comprehension, and writing. The home component helps the student build confidence and reinforce important reading strategies.

> **K-2 Literacy Intervention Programs provide support to CCSD 93 students who are underachieving in Language Arts skills with a goal of having all students be successful readers by the end of second grade by meeting or exceeding state standard measures.**

Blast Off: This program is offered to qualifying second-grade students first semester. Instruction is provided to small groups of students for twenty-five minutes each day. Each lesson focuses on helping the students to develop the strategies that readers and writers need to be successful. This is accomplished through the following components of the lesson: word recognition, rereading for fluency, reading of a new book, independent reading, writing, and word making. The home component helps the student build confidence and reinforce important reading strategies.

Stakeholder Connections

Teachers use ongoing assessment results to help make instructional decisions. Teachers also collaborate with Reading Specialists about student progress throughout the year.

Parents support literacy activities at home. Parents are invited to parent information meeting each semester.

Reading Specialist and trained Literacy Aides administer assessments throughout the year to determine if reading support is needed.

K-2 Literacy Aides work with identified students individually and in small groups.

Improvement Cycle

Reading Specialist, Curriculum Coordinator, Literacy Staff, teachers, students and parents provide feedback

---

Figure 30   K–2 literacy intervention programs.

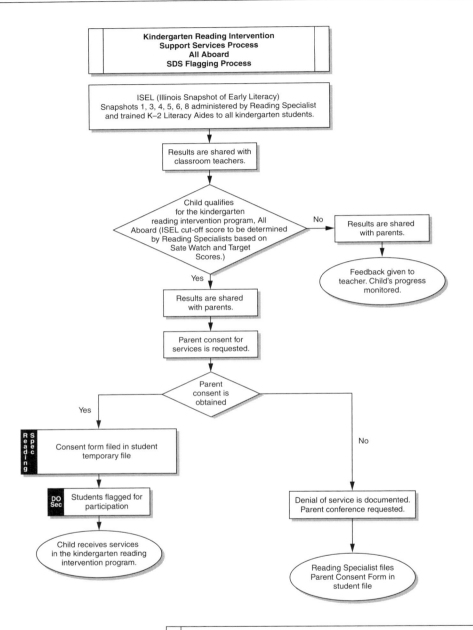

Figure 30 *Continued.*

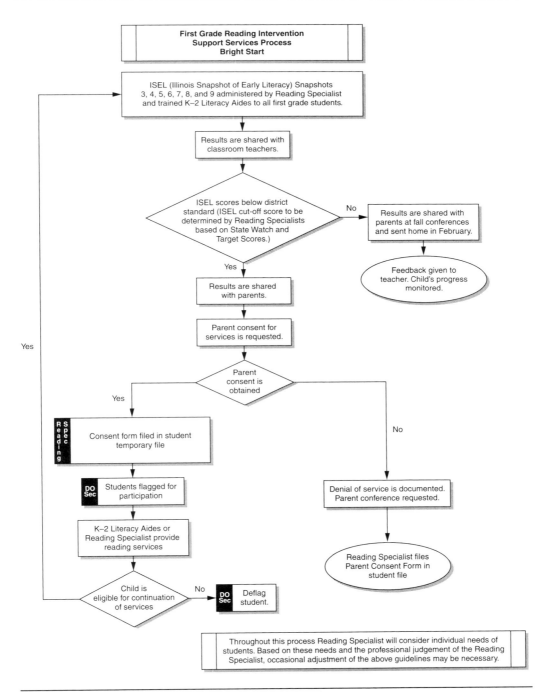

The flowchart contains the following elements:

First Grade Reading Intervention Support Services Process Bright Start

ISEL (Illinois Snapshot of Early Literacy) Snapshots 3, 4, 5, 6, 7, 8, and 9 administered by Reading Specialist and trained K–2 Literacy Aides to all first grade students.

Results are shared with classroom teachers.

ISEL scores below district standard (ISEL cut-off score to be determined by Reading Specialists based on State Watch and Target Scores.)

No → Results are shared with parents at fall conferences and sent home in February.

Feedback given to teacher. Child's progress monitored.

Yes

Results are shared with parents.

Parent consent for services is requested.

Parent consent is obtained

Yes

Reading Spec

Consent form filed in student temporary file

DO Sec

Students flagged for participation

K–2 Literacy Aides or Reading Specialist provide reading services

Child is eligible for continuation of services

No → DO Sec — Deflag student.

No

Denial of service is documented. Parent conference requested.

Reading Specialist files Parent Consent Form in student file

Yes

Throughout this process Reading Specialist will consider individual needs of students. Based on these needs and the professional judgement of the Reading Specialist, occasional adjustment of the above guidelines may be necessary.

Figure 30   *Continued.*

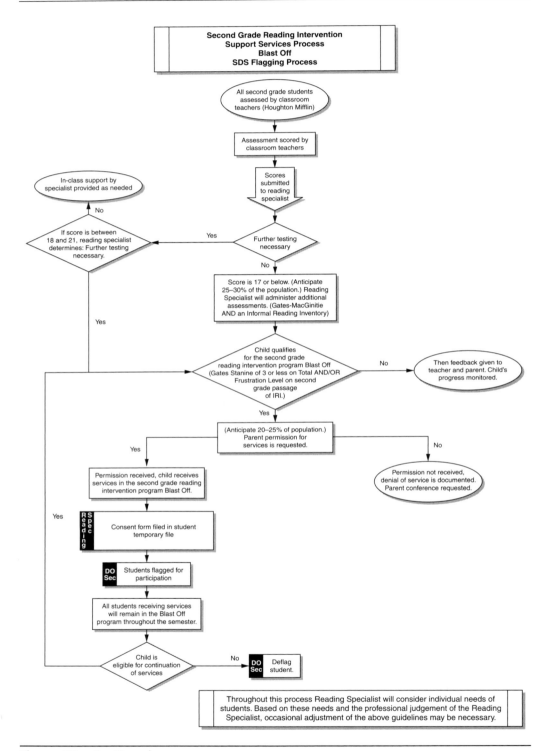

Figure 30 *Continued.*

Quality Process

Math Intervention Program

Community Consolidated School District 93 provides a Mathematics Intervention Program for student in grades 2-8. The goal of this program is to provide below grade level mathematics instruction to students who are performing below grade level in mathematics.

This instruction is provided via different models in elementary and middle school. In all cases, this program provides additional math instruction and is not a replacement of the grade level math program.

Elementary Math Intervention Program
(Grades 2-5)
- Daily, 30 minute sessions
- Instruction is provided by trained math aides
- Progress is reported
- In addition to grade level mathematics instruction

Middle School Math Intervention Program
(Grades 6-8)
- Daily class
- Taught by certified mathematics teachers
- Progress is reported
- In addition to grade level mathematics instruction

The Math Intervention program addresses three strategic themes. The first theme is Student Learning, the second is Stakeholder Satisfaction, and the third is Alignment of Support Systems.

Formative NWEA assessments are administered three times during the school year to determine performance and growth levels in mathematics. This data is considered along with other available formative and summative scores. Consistent below grade level performance on the above assessment is used by teachers to recommend students for math intervention services.

Parents/guardians of students recommended for Math Intervention receive notification of recommendation for placement and are requested to provide consent to provide Math Intervention Services. Once parental/guardian consent is received, student schedules are changed to allow for participation in the additional math instruction.

Students continue in Math Intervention until one of the following occurs:

- Satisfactory performance in Math Intervention
                                AND
- The student scores at grade level two consecutive times on NWEA
                                OR
- The parent or guardian requests the student be removed from the program

Stakeholder Connections

CCSD93 Board of Education approves the usage of funds to allow for implementation of this program.

Classroom teachers monitor student performance and refer students for Math Intervention.

Math Intervention teachers and aides monitor and report student progress to classroom teachers, students, and parents/guardians.

Parents/guardians provide consent for student to participate in Math Intervention.

Students engage in and self reflect about their progress in Math Intervention.

Improvement Cycle

Math Intervention program data is shared annually with the Board of Education.

Figure 31   Math intervention program.

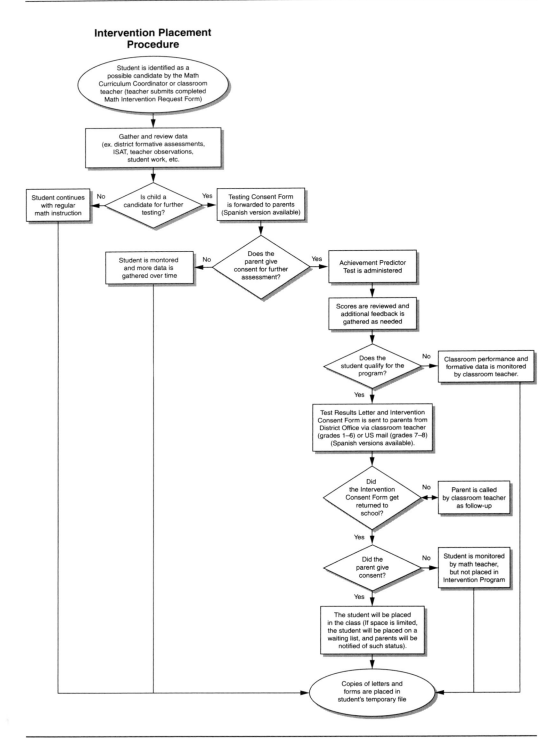

Intervention Placement Procedure

Figure 31 *Continued.*

Quality Process

Student Referral for Special Education Services

The state and federal regulations governing special education indicate that when there is reason to believe that a child may have a disability requiring special education and related services, the child shall be referred for special education services. The law provides that each school district shall develop and make known to all concerned persons the procedures by which an evaluation may be requested.

Community Consolidated School District 93 has a Special Service Team (SST) at each school, which comprises a building administrator, psychologist, social worker, resource consultant, speech/language pathologist, and school nurse. This team is responsible for processing referrals and documenting what action should be taken, as well as initiating the necessary procedures. The SST determines whether the referred child requires a Full and Individual Evaluation. Most self-contained programs (Preschool, Instructional, Guided, and so on) have their own SST that addresses the needs of only those children in that particular program.

Referrals may be made by any concerned person including, but not limited to, school personnel, the parent(s) of a child, an employee of a community service agency, another professional having knowledge of a child's problems, a child, or an employee of the State Board of Education. Staff development regarding the referral process is provided at the building level by the Special Service Team(s) on an annual basis. Referral procedures are outlined annually to parents through the District 93 Community Calendar. Preschool screening is held nine days per year from September through March for those students ages 33 months through 5 years of age. Preschool Screenings are advertised in the local newspapers, in PTA newsletters across the district and via correspondence to the private preschool in the area.

Figure 32 Student referral for special education services.

Determination of Instructional Placement

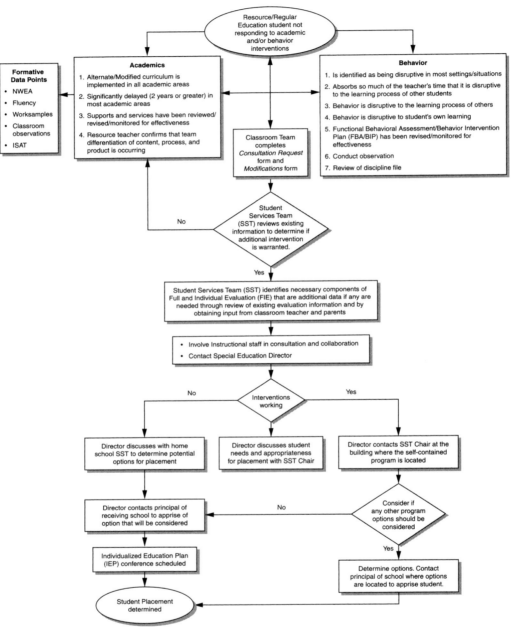

Figure 32 *Continued.*

CCSD93
Working together, nurturing the potential

Quality Process

Stakeholder Connections

Staff development regarding the referral process is provided at the building-level by the Special Service Team(s) on an annual basis.

Improvement Cycle

The referral process is reviewed triennially or as procedural mandates occur.

Section 504 Referral and Evaluation Procedures

Section 504 of the Rehabilitation Act has been in effect since 1973. For many years, its' primary focus has been in the area of employment for individuals with a handicap. However, within the last several years the Office for Civil Rights (OCR) had become proactive in the field of education of handicapped individuals. All individuals who are disabled under the Individuals with Disabilities Education Act (IDEA) are also considered to be handicapped and therefore protected under Section 504. However, all individuals who have been determined to be handicapped under Section 504 may not be disabled under IDEA.

If a district has reason to believe that, because of a handicap as defined under Section 504, a student needs either special accommodations or related services in the regular setting in order to participate in the school program, the district must evaluate the student. Section 504 protects all handicapped students, defined as those having any physical of mental impairment that substantially limits one ore more major life activities (including learning). If the student is determined to be handicapped under Section 504, the district must develop and implement a plan identifying the appropriate modifications and accommodations. These steps must be taken even though the student is not covered by the IDEA special education provision and procedures.

The Mission of CCSD 93 Student Services strives to maximize the academic, social, and emotional potential of each student by utilizing world-class educational practices, in partnership with parents, staff and community and to provide for the individual needs of the students.

What is required for the Section 504 evaluation and placement process is determined by the type of handicap suspected and the type of services the student may need. The evaluation must be sufficient to accurately and completely assess the nature and extent of the handicap and the recommended services.

The determination of what services are needed must be made by a group of persons knowledgeable about the student. The group should review the nature of the handicap, how it affects the student's education, whether specialized services are needed, and if so what those services are. The decisions about Section 504 eligibility and services must be documented in the student's file and reviewed periodically. Best practice would suggest to review information at least annually.

Reference:　*Code of Federal Regulations Part 104.3*
Community Consolidated School District 93 Policy
Cooperative Association for Special Education Policy 706.11

Figure 33　Section 504 referral and evaluation procedures.

Community Consolidated School District 93
Section 504 Evaluation Procedures

Team completes *Parent Notice
Consent for 504 Evaluation/Reevaluation*
form. It is the role of the SST to determine what
components/assessment are necessary to
make reasonable educational decisions
regarding the child.

The SST Chairperson or designee notifies the parent of the referral
and obtains signature on *Parent Notice Consent for 504 Evaluation/
Reevaluation* form. Parent is provided with a copy of the
*Parent/Student Rights in Identification, Evaluation, and Placement
Section 504 of the Rehabilitation Act of 1973.*

The SST Chairperson coordinates the gathering of relevant information
necessary to assist in the identification and/or justification of a possible
504 disability.

This may include any or all of the following:

    Present Levels of Performance from the classroom teacher

    Academic and/or General Intelligence Testing

    Report from School Nurse

    Report(s) from Related Service Personnel (OT, PT)

Within a reasonable time (usually parallel the sixty school days required in
special education) of the initiation of the referral, the SST Chairperson will
convene a Section 504 conference.

The *Section 504 Conference Notice* is forwarded to parent(s) and participants.

Participants may include any or all of the following individuals:

    • Building Principal or designee

    • Regular Education Teacher

    • Assessment Team Members

    • Parent/Guardian

    • Student

Discuss the information gathered and determine whether the student is
disabled under Section 504 and whether the identified disability substantially
limits one or more life activities.
Meeting is documented on *Section 504 Conference Summary* form.

Team identifies student's needs and
determines appropriate program
accomodations/services.
Document on *Section 504 Student
Accommodation Plan* form.

Yes → Student is
determined eligible for
Section 504
Plan.

No → Modifications remain in
place and student
progress is monitored.

Services are scheduled
and implemented.

Convene Annual Review to assess progress and determine if any
changes are warranted to Section 504 Plan.

Students should be reevaluated periodically. It is recommended
that a reevaluation be conducted at least every three years, though
not required. All previous components should be addressed.
Procedures for initial evaluation should be followed.

Figure 33   *Continued.*

Quality Process

Retention Procedures

Retention as expressed in our policy states that "the Principal will direct, monitor, and assist teachers in their evaluation of students and review grade assignments in order to insure uniformity of evaluation standards. A student's achievement of the skills for the grade to which he/she is assigned and his/her readiness for work at the next grade level will be assessed and evaluated before he/she is promoted." (725.02) Considerations that will be a part of the retention procedures are the Student Support Team (SST) Referral Process. That team is responsible for processing referrals, documenting what action should be taken, as well as initiating the necessary procedures. A consideration for retention should be addressed early in the process. Considerations for retention would be addressed if the SST has evaluated a student. Some questions the team asks are: is the student a second language learner, is the student a move-in or a former retained student, is this a new issue, the age of the student, has it been considered in the past, and when was the concern brought to the team. Retention concerns can be made by any concerned person including, but not limited to, school personnel, the parent(s) of a child, another professional having knowledge of the child, or an employee of the State Board of Education. Staff development regarding the referral process is provided at the building level on an annual basis. Parent will be notified immediately when concern is raised as noted in the SST referral process. Summer programming for middle school students is considered. Any student (grade 6, 7, or 8) who fails a course (failing grade [F] all 4 quarters) is a candidate for retention.

Figure 34　Retention procedures.

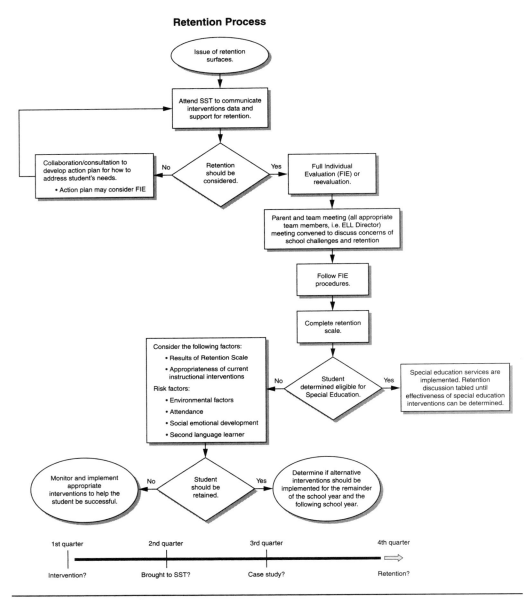

Figure 34   *Continued.*

Quality Process

Stranger Danger

The safety of students is a very high priority in Community Consolidated School District 93. Prevention programs are in place to provide students with strategies to implement if they feel they are in an unsettling situation. The Quality Process that follows is intended to outline the steps the district/school administrators will follow should a Stranger Danger case be reported. If a case is determined to warrant police investigation, the district staff will work collaboratively with their respective police department to bring the situation to resolve. Also outlined are the necessary communications to include staff, parents, students and other relevant stakeholders who have a need to know.

Community Consolidated School District 93 strives to maximize the academic, social, and emotional potential of each student by utilizing world-class educational practices, in partnership with parents, staff, and community.

This quality process links with the district mission as we work to ensure student safety so they can be focused on learning.

Figure 35 Stranger danger.

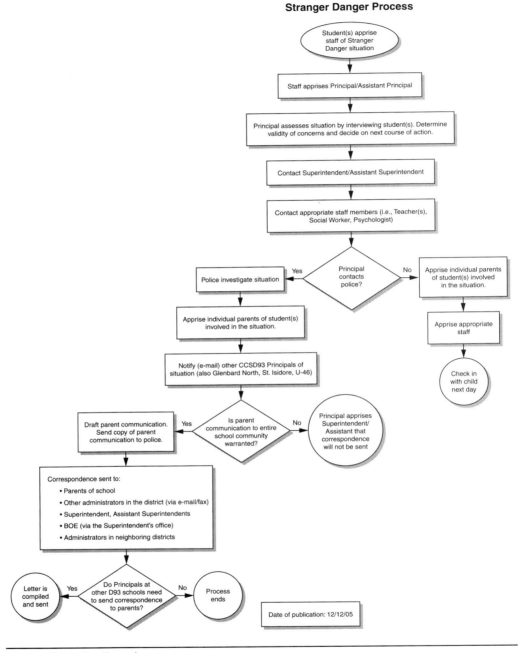

Stranger Danger Process

Student(s) apprise staff of Stranger Danger situation

Staff apprises Principal/Assistant Principal

Principal assesses situation by interviewing student(s). Determine validity of concerns and decide on next course of action.

Contact Superintendent/Assistant Superintendent

Contact appropriate staff members (i.e., Teacher(s), Social Worker, Psychologist)

Principal contacts police?

Yes → Police investigate situation

No → Apprise individual parents of student(s) involved in the situation.

Apprise appropriate staff

Check in with child next day

Apprise individual parents of student(s) involved in the situation.

Notify (e-mail) other CCSD93 Principals of situation (also Glenbard North, St. Isidore, U-46)

Is parent communication to entire school community warranted?

Yes → Draft parent communication. Send copy of parent communication to police.

No → Principal apprises Superintendent/Assistant that correspondence will not be sent

Correspondence sent to:
- Parents of school
- Other administrators in the district (via e-mail/fax)
- Superintendent, Assistant Superintendents
- BOE (via the Superintendent's office)
- Administrators in neighboring districts

Do Principals at other D93 schools need to send correspondence to parents?

Yes → Letter is compiled and sent

No → Process ends

Date of publication: 12/12/05

Figure 35   *Continued.*

STANDARDS-BASED INSTRUCTIONAL PROCESS

The Standards-Based Instructional Process is the most important flowchart example we have in the book. When it comes to process management, there are certain processes that have greater importance than others, and the instruction process is at the top. Most educators would consider instruction to be a system because it usually includes the direct instruction of students, the curriculum that is taught, and assessments used to measure the amount of knowledge learned and the ability to apply what is learned. Some would also include classroom management as part of the instructional system. Separate out instruction and you have a specific process that arguably contributes the most value to the instructional system. The question is, what does developing an instruction process mean and how do you deploy it? The next set of four flowcharts (Figures 36 through 39) offer specific suggestions about how an instructional process could be designed, followed by deployment documents.

It would seem intuitive that instruction is the most influential process in education if we are talking about student academic achievement, yet we would venture a guess based on experience that this educational process is more poorly managed than any other. There is a whole area of statistics devoted to "value added" research that has been well established over the last two decades, mostly by Dr. William L. Sanders at the Value-Added Research and Assessment Center at the University of Tennessee. This mixed-model methodology collects longitudinal data of individual student achievement that can be matched with individual teachers and looks at achievement gains. Gain scores can be associated with a teacher, giving him or her credit, so to speak, for that gain. This allows other factors such as socioeconomic level, class size, expenditures, previous grades and test scores, and teacher degrees, to be factored in to see how much effect they have on learning.

For example, if we know an individual teacher and how many students he or she has and we know this information for a large group of teachers and students, then we could see if class size is a predictor of student academic progress. Turns out, it isn't. Because they can identify student variables such as socioeconomic level, they can analyze the data to see of that is a good predictor of student academic progress. Most educators would say yes, that is, the lower the socioeconomic level, the poorer the student academic progress. Turns out, that isn't true either. *What's the best determinant of student academic progress? The effectiveness of the teacher.*

Robert Marzano has continued this effect size approach to identifying variables that accelerate or impede academic achievement. Marzano's research is highlighted here because he is one of the most significant educational researchers of our time. The body of work he has created is enormous and it has passed both peer reviews and the approval of teacher practitioners throughout the world. (Note: One of the authors was a colleague of Marzano at the Mid-Continent Research for Education and Learning (McREL) educational laboratory.) Marzano says that schools can have a tremendous impact on student achievement if they follow the direction provided by the research. The instructional flowchart is an example of what he means by following the direction provided by the research. Another point he makes is that highly effective schools produce

1. Making sure the standard is taught

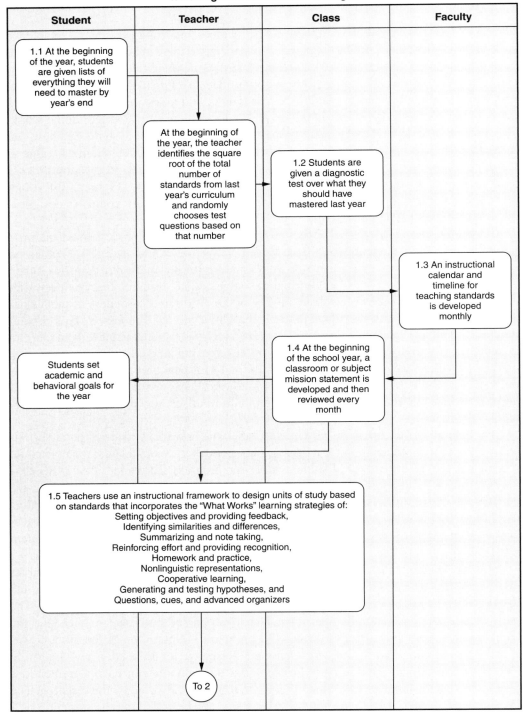

Figure 36   Making sure the standard is taught.

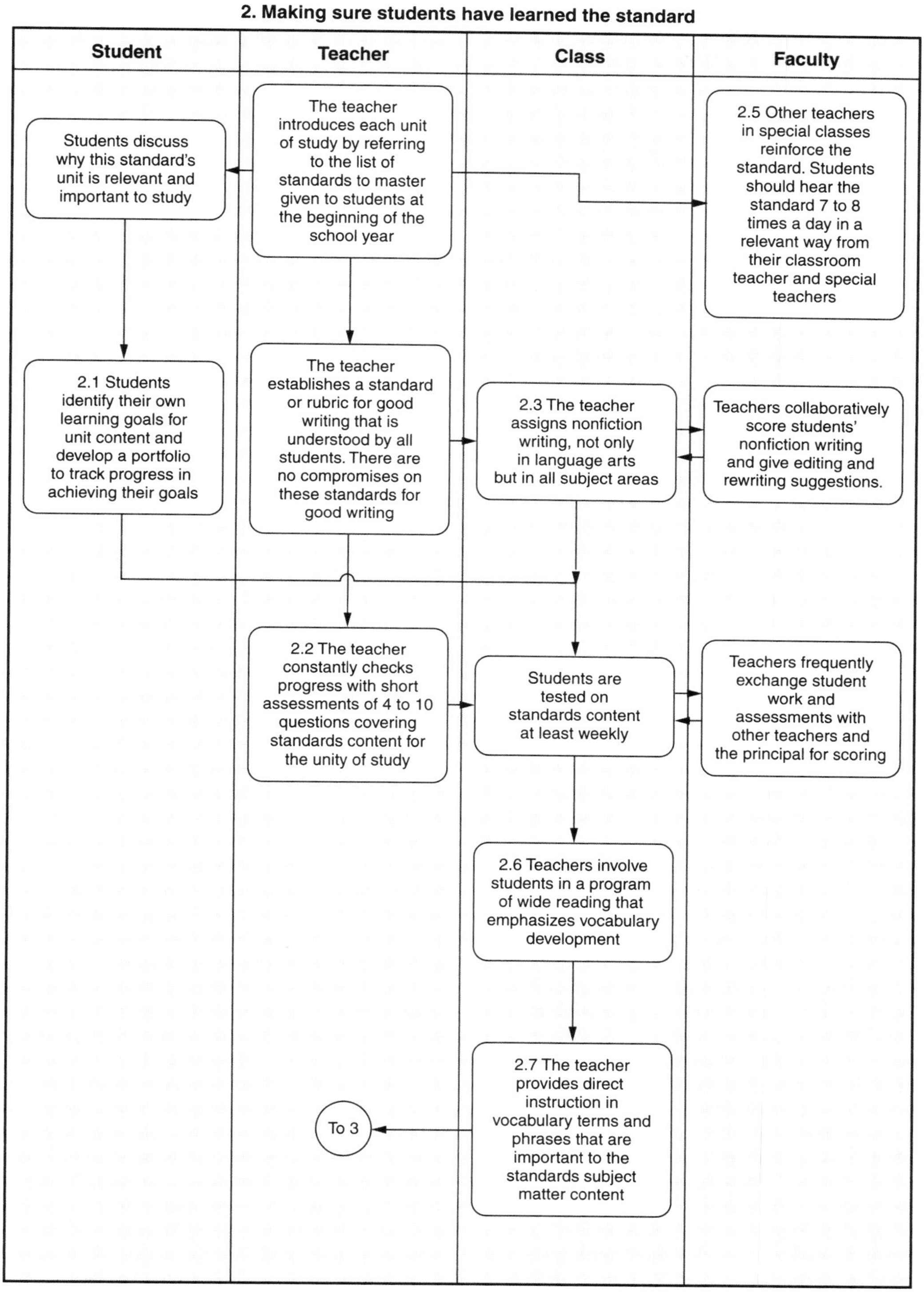

2. Making sure students have learned the standard

Student	Teacher	Class	Faculty

The teacher introduces each unit of study by referring to the list of standards to master given to students at the beginning of the school year

Students discuss why this standard's unit is relevant and important to study

2.5 Other teachers in special classes reinforce the standard. Students should hear the standard 7 to 8 times a day in a relevant way from their classroom teacher and special teachers

2.1 Students identify their own learning goals for unit content and develop a portfolio to track progress in achieving their goals

The teacher establishes a standard or rubric for good writing that is understood by all students. There are no compromises on these standards for good writing

2.3 The teacher assigns nonfiction writing, not only in language arts but in all subject areas

Teachers collaboratively score students' nonfiction writing and give editing and rewriting suggestions.

2.2 The teacher constantly checks progress with short assessments of 4 to 10 questions covering standards content for the unity of study

Students are tested on standards content at least weekly

Teachers frequently exchange student work and assessments with other teachers and the principal for scoring

2.6 Teachers involve students in a program of wide reading that emphasizes vocabulary development

To 3

2.7 The teacher provides direct instruction in vocabulary terms and phrases that are important to the standards subject matter content

Figure 37   Making sure students have learned the standard.

3. Making sure students who didn't learn the standard, learn it

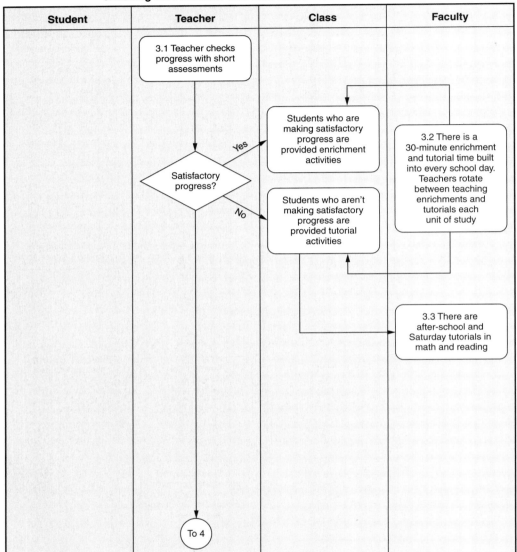

Figure 38   Making sure students who didn't learn the standard, learn it.

results that *almost entirely overcome the effects of student background.* If value-added research has isolated the effectiveness of the teacher as the best determinant of student academic progress, and Marzano and others identify many of the practices that make a teacher effective, then it would seem logical to design an instructional process incorporating as many of these researched variables as possible and appropriate. *The point Marzano is making is that there needs to be a commonly decided and developed*

4. Making sure students do not forget what they have learned

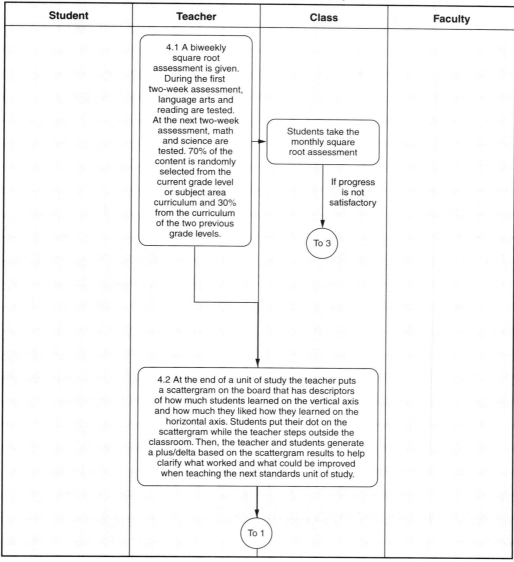

Student	Teacher	Class	Faculty

4.1 A biweekly square root assessment is given. During the first two-week assessment, language arts and reading are tested. At the next two-week assessment, math and science are tested. 70% of the content is randomly selected from the current grade level or subject area curriculum and 30% from the curriculum of the two previous grade levels.

Students take the monthly square root assessment

If progress is not satisfactory

To 3

4.2 At the end of a unit of study the teacher puts a scattergram on the board that has descriptors of how much students learned on the vertical axis and how much they liked how they learned on the horizontal axis. Students put their dot on the scattergram while the teacher steps outside the classroom. Then, the teacher and students generate a plus/delta based on the scattergram results to help clarify what worked and what could be improved when teaching the next standards unit of study.

To 1

Figure 39   Making sure students do not forget what they have learned.

framework (system) of effective teaching. When we talk about teaching, what do we agree are the components and activities that describe effective teaching? How would we visually design what effective teaching looks like? Can we agree on the basic components of an effective teaching process?

You can approach the development of an instructional process by looking at what the research says should be included or you can look for examples of instructional processes that are creating results that you think are worthy of replication or modification. You obviously can do both, and the example we have developed uses research and benchmarking to gather the components and activities that comprise the process.

WORLD-CLASS EDUCATIONAL PRACTICES APPLIED TO STANDARDS-BASED INSTRUCTIONAL PROCESSES (CLASSROOM FOCUS)

Deployment Flowchart: Standards-Based Instruction

The four standards' instructional questions are based on the work of Michael White, PhD, who is a professional development associate with the Center for Performance Assessment and the director of Educational Consulting Services, an educational organization in Cincinnati, Ohio. The content under each of the four questions comes from world-class practices and researched applications found in Baldrige Award–winning school districts, 90/90/90 Schools, W. E. Deming's principles of continuous improvement and learning as translated for educators by Lee Jenkins in *Improving Student Learning* and *Permission to Forget,* the Marzano *What Works in Schools* series and his recent book titled *The Art and Science of Teaching,* the Pathfinder materials, the *World Class Schools* series, and the mastery learning concepts found in the *Models of Teaching* book. This standards-based instructional flowchart is obviously not meant to be an exhaustive synthesis of instructional literature and practice. It is also not meant to be the only way to configure instructional best practice into a flowchart, even though it is clear that if instruction were conducted as the flowcharts describe, student achievement in any setting would be excellent, and the achievement gap would be significantly reduced or eliminated. It is meant to stimulate discussion about best practice in instruction among administrators and teachers. Flowcharting the instructional process makes that discussion much more exact and creates new levels of understanding about what instructional best practices look like in the classroom. (Note: In the flowchart you will notice the use of square root measurement. This concept comes from W. Edwards Deming and is wonderfully illustrated in Lee Jenkins's book titled *Improving Student Learning,* published by ASQ Quality Press. The idea is to sample students' knowledge of what has been taught by identifying the total number of facts, concepts, principles, formulas, or whatever else they have been taught, and then periodically testing them based on the square root of that total number each time. As Jenkins [2003] states, "The square root provides a large enough sample size to be accurate. The sample size is large enough if quizzing is done every week or every other week.")

Simulated Teacher Dialogue Related to Flowchart Steps

1.1 *"Students, this is what you will be expected to know by the end of this (grade, subject, semester, and so on). This is what you will need to master to be successful in the next (grade, subject, post high school education, and so on)."*

1.2 *"Students, I want to know what you know. Remember that your teacher(s) (last year, last semester, and so on) told you that what you learned was so important that you would want to remember it. I want to give you a chance to show me what you learned and what you remember from (last year, last semester, and so on). This is not a test that I am going to grade but it is very important because I don't know where to start this class until you show me what you know."*

1.4 *"Students, I want you to be clear about what my job is as your teacher and what your job is as a student. My job is to make sure you know exactly what is expected of you in this class. That is why I gave you the list of standards at the beginning of this class that you will be expected to master by the end of this (grade, class, and so on). It is also my job to make sure you understand what the quality of your work should look like to meet or exceed my expectations. I will do that by showing and posting examples of quality work, especially writing examples. I will also teach you what you need to know to master and remember the standards. And students, let me be very clear about this, I am not giving you permission to forget anything we learn in this class. You will be held accountable/responsible for all of the content you are taught. Lastly, it is my job to keep you enthused about learning this content. It will be your job as a student to be responsible for your own learning. To help you be responsible for your own learning, it is important for us to develop a statement for this class that gives us a focus* (usually something that says to continuously improve until we have mastered the content of the class) *and describes how we will cooperate with each other in order to be successful. You will be developing your own goals and keeping track of how well you are learning and remembering the standards because that is what responsible learners do."*

2.1 *"Students, I have already said that what responsible learners do is set learning goals and keep track of how well you are doing so that you will know when you have achieved your learning goals. As we begin each (lesson, unit of study, standard, and so on) you will set a learning goal and develop a tracking sheet to record how well you are doing in achieving that goal. We will also track how well the class is doing by recording our progress on the chart posted on the wall. This will help us assess how well we are doing in accomplishing our focus statement and how well we are cooperating with each other so that we can all be successful."*

2.3 *"Students, let's see what we have learned so far. Please tell me what standard we are learning in this unit. I'm going to ask you a few questions to see what we know about this standard. Please write your answer using our good writing rubric. Why are we doing this? That's right, because we develop logical thinking and understand our reasoning better by writing out and justifying our answers, even in subjects like science and mathematics. What is our classroom focus/goal? Yes, it is to continuously improve, and this little review test will help us find out how much we have improved since last time."*

2.6 *"Students, when you are doing silent reading in class or at home, identify new words you find interesting or don't know. Write these words on a small piece of paper and mark the page in the book where the word is, using the slip of paper. When you finish reading, go back and try to figure out the meaning of these words using the information and clues surrounding the word. If you are not sure, make your best guess. Write about or draw a picture of each word and your guess in your personal vocabulary notebook. We will be using these words in class so that we can better learn what they mean."*

4.1 *"Students, now we are going to do our biweekly 'Are We Remembering What We Have Learned Test.' Will (name a student) find the square root of (number of concepts needed to be mastered) and then run the random number generator. Class, why do we do this test? Yes, because I said at the very beginning of this class that you don't have permission to forget anything we learn and because what you learn in this class is important to know for your next (class, subject, post graduate work, and so on) and forever. Remembering what we have learned is as important as learning new things."*

4.2 *"Students, I have told you many times that I have two goals for this class. The first is to make sure you are ready to be successful for the next (grade, class, post graduate experience, and so on) by mastering and remembering the list of content I gave you at the beginning of this (grade, class, and so on). My second goal is equally important to me and that is to keep or hopefully increase your enthusiasm for learning this content. That is why we always review how much you think you learned and how much you liked how you learned at the end of each (unit, standard, and so on). Please put your dot on the scattergram where you believe what you learned and how much you liked how you learned come together, or intersect. Be prepared to do a plus/delta about what went well and what could be improved so I can work on what you would like to see us do in this class to help you learn more and to make it more interesting."*

WORLD-CLASS EDUCATIONAL PRACTICES APPLIED TO STANDARDS-BASED INSTRUCTIONAL PROCESSES (SCHOOL FOCUS)

I. Making Sure the Standard Is Taught

1. School improvement plan data (charts, graphs, trend lines, and so on) are on display in very visible parts of the school. Charts, graphs, and tables that display current student achievement information as well as data about the continuous improvement that students are making are also on display in the principal's office and on walls in the halls, lunch room, and other visible places throughout the school. Trophy cases should be full of exemplary student academic work, including essays that meet or exceed the school writing rubric standards, science projects, social studies papers, and outstanding examples of mathematics work. It would be clear to anyone walking the halls of the school that there is a "laser-like" focus on continuous improvement of student academic achievement. (Baldrige schools, 90/90/90 schools, and many other schools.)

2. The content considered essential for all students at each grade level or subject area, including books to be read and projects, like research papers, to be developed, is

displayed or posted in public places to further reinforce the "laser-like" focus on continuous improvement of student academic achievement. (The district curriculum department has identified and communicated the content considered essential for all students versus that considered supplemental or nice to know but not necessary to know. Additionally, there has been an assessment by district curriculum directors to guarantee that the essential content can be taught in the amount of time available for instruction for the year.) (Deming principles as translated by Lee Jenkins in *Improving Student Learning* and *Permission to Forget.*)

3. The district prepares printed lists of the standards students will need to secure (only the secure standards) by the end of a grade or subject area and hands those to teachers at the beginning of the school year. (Deming principles as translated by Lee Jenkins in *Improving Student Learning* and *Permission to Forget.*)

4. At the beginning of the year there is an academic pep rally staged with the same enthusiasm as if the school was preparing for a state-level sporting event. During the rally, there is a story (like those in the Pathfinder materials) or an actual presentation by a person who overcame great odds through effort and will. The two messages that students leave the academic pep rally with are that this school takes pride in the academic achievement of its students and that what makes a difference in achievement is effort and not ability. Quotes that emphasize effort are found throughout the school and during announcements and in publications. This message is especially important to convey to parents, who are often the greatest believers in the myth of ability over effort. (Marzano in the *What Works in Schools* and *Pathfinder* books and materials. Practice used in many schools that are considered high performers. Also practices described in *World Class Elementary Schools* by Richard Haynes and Donald Chalker.)

5. The principal establishes ways to monitor the school-level factors that have the highest impact student on achievement. These are, in order of their effect on student achievement: guaranteed and viable curriculum, challenging goals and effective feedback, parental and community involvement, safe and orderly environment, and collegiality and professionalism. (Marzano in the *What Works in Schools* series.)

6. The principal establishes a norm of staff collegiality and professionalism by reinforcing the practice of grade-level or subject area teachers developing monthly instructional calendars. (Marzano in the *What Works in Schools* series, PDSA instructional cycle developed and applied in many schools.)

7. The principal establishes a norm of staff collegiality and professionalism through teacher supplier and customer conversations. These conversations occur in October for the purpose of customer teachers describing to supplier teachers (4th grade teachers to 3rd grade teachers, for example) how well students were prepared for success in the next grade or subject area and how well they retained what they had learned. Discussions are for the purpose of helping supplier teachers better prepare students to be successful and not for the purpose of judging or evaluating others. (Deming and the process management literature.)

8. The principal establishes a norm of staff collegiality and professionalism through the use of student and staff focus groups. These focus groups occur in October or November in the designated receiver school. The purpose of the focus groups is to receive feedback about how well students were prepared to be successful at the next school and how well they retained what they had learned. Estimates would be gathered at this time from the receiver school staff about the amount of classroom time that was needed at the beginning of the school year to review last year's content. (Baldrige schools.)

II. Making Sure Students Have Learned the Standard

1. The principal leads the teaching staff through a process that examines data trends using disaggregated data by subgroup performance and by subtest performance. There is an expectation set for high academic performance and this expectation holds true for all subgroups in the school. There is an agreement among staff that all subgroups of students should achieve the same high expectations for academic performance. The data trends and expectations set the stage for the *school improvement plan* process. (NCLB.)

2. The principal establishes a norm for continuous improvement by helping staff understand that processes and not people cause almost all performance gaps. Part of that norm is an analysis of process stability and capability through the use of control charts and histograms. This process analysis is developed for each academic subject area and for discipline incidents. Common and special cause related to process stability becomes part of the language staff use in the school. Standardizing, stabilizing, reducing variation, and streamlining processes are always the focus of improvement efforts. This understanding of how processes work is used to better understand and improve classroom processes. (Deming principles as translated by Lee Jenkins in *Improving Student Learning* and *Permission to Forget*.)

3. The principal establishes a norm of staff collegiality and professionalism with an expectation that a regular assessment strategy is the frequent external scoring of student work. This means that on a regular basis teachers exchange student work and assessments with other teachers for scoring, teachers exchange student work and assessments with a teacher or teachers at the next grade level, and teachers give student work and assessments to the principal for review and/or scoring. (90/90/90 schools as described by Douglas Reeves at the Center for Performance Assessment.)

4. The principal leads the development of an instructional framework that teachers use to design units of study that incorporates the research-based strategies of: identifying similarities and differences, summarizing and note taking, reinforcing effort and providing recognition, homework and practice, nonlinguistic representations, cooperative learning, setting objectives and providing feedback, generating and testing hypotheses, and questions, cues, and advance organizers. (Marzano in *Classroom Instruction That Works* from the *What Works in Schools* research.)

5. The principal schedules and supports a program of wide reading, including silent sustained reading (SSR), that emphasizes vocabulary development so that students

build their background knowledge capacity and improve their academic achievement. (Marzano in *Building Background Knowledge for Academic Achievement* from the *What Works in Schools* research.)

6. The principal reinforces the teaching practices of direct instruction in vocabulary terms and phrases that are essential to the mastery and retention of specific subject matter content so that students build background knowledge specific to that subject area and improve academic achievement in that subject area. The principal understands that because of the powerful influence this practice has on understanding content knowledge, especially for students whose academic achievement is being significantly affected by the lack of background knowledge, this practice can not be left up to the individual decisions of teachers to use or not use. Also, the principal reinforces the practice by saying that a very important component of content instruction is to determine the essential vocabulary for their subject areas and/or grade levels. This determination is done with all grade-level or subject area teachers together so that the essential vocabulary is taught uniformly across grades and subjects. These decisions about essential vocabulary are directed by district and state curriculum standards. Determining what content vocabulary to teach becomes part of teacher discussions when they develop their monthly instructional calendar. (Marzano in *Building Background Knowledge for Academic Achievement* from the *What Works in Schools* research.)

III. Making Sure Students Who Didn't Learn the Standard, Learn It

1. The principal schedules 30 minutes of time each day for tutorial and enrichment activities in reading and mathematics. The principal establishes an expectation that during this time all teachers in the building will be working with a small group of students on reading or mathematics to help them learn what they need to learn or extend what they have already learned. Teachers will rotate at appropriate times from being a tutorial to an enrichment teacher. During this 30-minute time, nothing else is scheduled so that all teachers are available to teach and all students are available to learn. (PDSA instructional cycle from Baldrige schools, the mastery learning literature, for example, *Models of Teaching* by Joyce and Weil, and 90/90/90 school practices described by Douglas Reeves.)

2. Elementary principals state to teachers in very direct terms that reading is the most important subject in this school and that making sure students read at or above grade level is the most important goal to accomplish. Elementary principals give teachers permission to neglect other subjects, especially social studies and science, in order to devote the time necessary to assure that all students are readers. This priority is firmly supported by district senior leaders. (Baldrige school district practices, 90/90/90 school practices described by Douglas Reeves and the Education Trust Foundation.)

3. Middle and high school principals emphasize that all teachers are teachers of reading and that reading in the content areas is one of the most important skill sets teachers need to have. New hires must demonstrate that they have reading in the content area

skill sets as a prerequisite for employment in this school. Middle and high school principals state to teachers in very direct terms that reading is the most important subject in this school and that making sure students read at or above grade level is the most important goal to accomplish. (Extrapolation of 90/90/90 school descriptions and middle/high school research.)

4. The principal has a weekly updated list of academically at-risk students. He or she knows if those students are making adequate progress. If they are, continued adequate progress for those students should be reported to the principal monthly. For students who aren't making adequate progress, there is a discussion between the student, teacher, and principal to identify the root causes of inadequate progress. A research-based instructional approach(es) to remedy the learning gap(s) is identified that addresses root causes, and the approach is implemented immediately. Students are also asked about how they like to learn so that student enthusiasm for learning can be increased. Progress should be assessed for these students weekly and reported to the principal at the end of each week. The principal randomly draws students from this list on Friday and sits with them to briefly assess academic progress for the week by asking them to read or discuss what they have learned. (90/90/90 school practices as described by Douglas Reeves, and PDSA instructional cycle as practiced in Baldrige schools.)

5. The principal facilitates a volunteer mentor program to directly increase the number and quality of broad life experiences students have, especially for those students who come to school with deficits in background knowledge. (Marzano in *Building Background Knowledge for Academic Achievement* from the *What Works in Schools* research.)

IV. Making Sure Students Do Not Forget What They Have Learned

1. The principal establishes an expectation among the teaching staff that retention of what is learned is as important as learning it. (Deming principles as translated by Lee Jenkins in *Improving Student Learning* and *Permission to Forget.*)

2. The principal periodically does a square root assessment over essential content by choosing students randomly from the student population, making sure that subgroups of students are proportionally represented in the assessment group. These square root assessments are done individually and in small groups. (Deming principles as translated by Lee Jenkins in *Improving Student Learning* and *Permission to Forget.*)

3. Alternatively, the principal, with central office assistance, sets up a short-cycle assessment process where grade-level assessments are given four times a year, each assessment measures the degree of mastery of *all* the secure content for that grade level, the September and May assessments are the same, the November and February assessments are alternative forms of the same assessment, all assessments are built using the state assessment format, assessments are administered "whole-group," the September assessment is used for baseline data and to help the teacher to know where to begin instruction, each quarterly assessment is used to track student growth during the year

and to guide instructional improvements, assessment results are shared with students, and assessment results are not used for grades. (Baldrige schools and Deming.)

4. The principal establishes a professional learning community through the use of the *whole faculty study group* process. Specifically, teacher conversations during grade-level collaboration time focus on essential questions like, "How do we teach so that students better comprehend what they read?" Teachers use the PDSA continuous improvement cycle to *plan* according to data indicating that students need to improve _____. They *try out* their plan by agreeing that when teaching they will _____. They *study* student results to see if learning has increased and understanding has deepened. Lastly, teachers *act* to systematically incorporate what works into their teaching. Teachers use this four-step process during the entire school year, over and over again, so that a norm of continuous improvement and professional collaboration is constantly reinforced. (Deming, and Murphy and Lick as described in *Whole-Faculty Study Groups,* Second Edition.)

ELL Variations

1. First, give English language learners extra time and instruction in literacy, either through longer school days or extended years.

2. Second, assign the best teachers to English language learners and provide professional development in effective teaching strategies.

3. Third, use proven techniques for teaching basic word recognition skills, including phonics and phonological awareness.

4. Fourth, provide lots of practice reading and frequent assessments to pinpoint children's reading strengths and weaknesses.

5. Fifth, provide structured academic conversation built around books and other subject matter activities to build vocabulary and comprehension.

6. Sixth, provide several years of intensive, high-quality instruction to help students master the vocabulary, comprehension, and oral language skills that will make them fully fluent in speaking, reading, and writing English.

(As described in *Research Points,* Winter 2004: Volume 2, Issue 1 published by the American Educational Research Association.)

STANDARDS-BASED INSTRUCTIONAL PROCESS MATRIX

The following matrix is an example of a check sheet that could be developed to track deployment activities for the standards-based instructional process. This matrix goes beyond initial deployment steps that would be tracked under the "standardize the

	Standardize the process	Stabilize the process	Reduce process variation	Streamline the process
Make sure the standard is taught				
Develop student lists of standards				
Develop grade-level or subject area diagnostic tests				
Develop monthly instructional calendars				
Schedule time for collaborative teacher planning				
Design units of study using the "What Works" learning strategies				
Make sure students have learned the standard				
Establish standards or rubics for measuring good writing				
Schedule time for collaborative scoring of student writing				
Schedule time for wide reading activities				
Design short assessment process				
Assessment data used to make instructional decisions				
Teacher teams review assessment data				

Figure 40   Standards-based instructional process matrix.

	Standardize the process	Stabilize the process	Reduce process variation	Streamline the process
Make sure students who didn't learn the standard, learn it				
Schedule daily 30-minute enrichment and tutorial time				
Create new tutorials				
Use different materials for enrichment				
Rotate teachers between enrichments and tutorials				
Make sure students do not forget what they have learned				
Build reviews and assessments of previously learned standards into the instructional calendar				
Use end-of-unit scattergrams				

Figure 40　*Continued.*

process" column to identify if the process owner, a principal in this case, is also working to improve the process by stabilizing it, reducing process variation, and streamlining the process.

The four examples, the classroom-level teaching to standards flowchart, the simulated teacher dialogue, the school-level descriptions of support activities related to the teaching to standards flowchart, and the standards-based instruction process matrix are all very useful deployment documents. We said earlier that the most important thing a process manager must contend with in deployment is to get what was in the designers' minds into the minds of the people who are going to use it exactly as it was designed. The flowchart, simulated dialogue, and school descriptions are examples of ways to communicate the essence of the design to the practitioner with as few misunderstandings as possible. Someone merely describing a new design would be the worst way to do this. Graphic descriptions are the best way. The matrix is a checklist for the person responsible for deploying the design to keep track of both deployment and improvement activities. Standardizing the process is the deployment step; stabilizing, reducing variation, and streamlining are improvement activities.

AT-RISK STUDENT PERFORMANCE IMPROVEMENT PROCESS

The flowchart depicted in Figure 41 was designed to address the issue of how to close the gap in academic performance between students. The flowchart addresses the question of what a process would look like that significantly reduces the variation between high and low achievers. When boards of education say that we want to close the gap in performance so that all students can achieve what they have the potential to achieve, the gap that they are referring to is really the variation of achievement scores across the student population. This gap is caused by variation built into the various instructional processes, which when added together (grade to grade, subject to subject), produce different levels of student achievement. The desire may be to close the gap, but the solution,

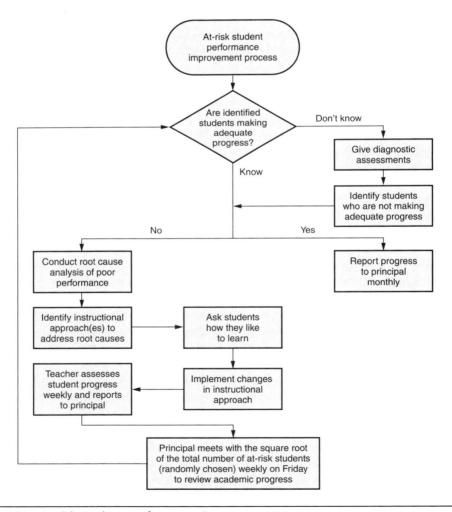

Figure 41 At-risk student performance improvement process.

as we have stated repeatedly, is to reduce process variation. This is no different than a superintendent's statement at the beginning of the book that said, "Everything we do that determines how well students succeed occurs in a system of interconnected processes, unacceptable variation exists in all those processes, and our key to successfully educating all students in the future is to understand and reduce that variation."

This *at-risk student performance improvement process* was designed by teachers and administrators using their own experience and a few appropriate benchmarks. The basic flowchart was designed over the course of an afternoon meeting and then field-tested. At first the Friday meetings with the principal were not part of the process. One principal on the team had started this practice and suggested it be incorporated into the design. It was, and the resulting improvement in student performance across the field sites confirmed its usefulness. The square root student selection process is the same process we have mentioned earlier that comes from a suggestion made by Lee Jenkins in his book *Improving Student Learning*. This improvement process was extremely effective in reducing the variation in student academic performance by bringing low performers much closer to the academic standards set by high-performing students.

Appendix A
School Customers

WHO ARE SCHOOL CUSTOMERS?

- Students
- Professional faculty
- Support staff
- Parents
- Community members
- Receiving school or schools
- World of work or businesses
- Institutes of higher education
- State and federal departments of education

WHAT DO THEY REQUIRE AND/OR EXPECT?

- Students require a caring, safe, and orderly learning environment.
- Students require a clear understanding about what constitutes acceptable and exceptional work.
- Students require knowing that they will be evaluated fairly.
- Students require clear behavioral expectations.
- Students need to be treated respectfully and fairly by faculty and staff.
- Students need clear descriptions of what they are expected to learn.
- Students expect to receive help when it is needed.
- Students need to learn in a socially supportive and interactive environment.
- Students expect to be satisfied (delighted) with their school experience.

- Students expect to be enthused about what is learned and how it is learned.

- Professional and support staff require a safe and secure work environment.

- Professional and support staff need to know how their jobs support the accomplishment of the district mission.

- Professional and support staff need to know how job performance is measured, evaluated, and rewarded.

- Professional and support staff need to know what constitutes ethical behavior and what the consequences of unethical behavior are.

- Professional and support staff need to know what high performance looks like and what goals and/or targets need to be achieved.

- Professional and support staff need to feel supported and respected by supervisors and peers.

- Professional and support staff need to receive help and support when requested.

- Professional and support staff need to be informed in a timely manner.

- Professional and support staff expect to be provided professional development that is relevant, of high quality, and aligned to job requirements.

- Professional and support staff expect to participate in decisions that directly affect their work.

- Receiving schools expect students to have the skills, knowledge, and an aptitude for learning that will make them successful at the next level of education.

- Parents require their son or daughter to learn in a safe, caring, orderly, and respectful environment.

- Parents need well-qualified teachers in every classroom.

- Parents expect their son or daughter to achieve his or her learning potential.

- Parents expect to be informed about issues, events, programs, and practices in a timely manner.

- Businesses expect students who are well prepared for the workplace of the 21st century.

- Institutes of higher education (trade schools, community colleges, colleges, and universities) expect students who are well prepared to be successful at the next level of education.

Appendix B

Example Process Management and Improvement Matrix

Core quality processes	Process owner	Process target	Acceptable process variation	Process measure	Is the process stable? (Predictable over time) Yes or no	Is the process capable? (Ability to meet or exceed expectations) Yes or no
Certified staff evaluation	WS	100% process compliance	No variation	Timeline and step checklist (sample)		
		100% rater reliability	No variation	Written evaluation reliability assessments		
		4.0 sigma efficiency (99%)		Sigma calculation		
Certified staff hiring	WS	100% process compliance	No variation	Timeline and step checklist (sample)		
		100% profile match	–5 profile attributes	Completed profile attribute list		
		First-year teachers' students meet or exceed RIT growth targets in: Reading (all goal strands) Mathematics (all goal strands)	+ or – 1 standard deviation	NWEA typical growth to actual growth		
ELL referral	MK	100% identification process compliance	No variation	Timeline and step checklist		
ESL/ bilingual	MK	Exited ELL students meet/ exceed reading and mathematics growth targets	No variation	NWEA typical growth to actual growth		

Core quality processes	Process owner	Process target	Acceptable process variation	Process measure	**Is the process stable?** (Predictable over time) yes or no	**Is the process capable?** (Ability to meet or exceed expectations) yes or no
IDSA level 2	KF	100% identification process compliance 90% parent satisfaction	No variation + or − 1 standard deviation from target	Timeline and step checklist + or − 1 standard deviation from target		
IDSA level 3	KF	100% identification process compliance 90% parent satisfaction	No variation + or − 1 standard deviation from target	Timeline and step checklist Satisfaction survey XmR chart		
K–2 literacy intervention	CB	100% process (K, 1, 2) compliance Participating students are successful readers by the end of second grade	No variation Meet or exceed state standards	Timeline and step checklist State standard measures		
Math intervention	LP	100% intervention placement process compliance After intervention student meets/ exceeds mathematics RIT growth targets	No variation + or − 1 standard deviation from target	Timeline and step checklist NWEA typical growth to actual growth		
Preschool referral	MS	100% process compliance with step 1 part B and step 2 95% parent satisfaction with referral process	No variation + or − 1 standard deviation from target	Timeline and step checklist Interview or survey XmR chart		
Preschool transition	MS	100% process compliance 95% parent satisfaction with transition	No variation + or − 1 standard deviation from target	Timeline and step checklist Interview or survey XmR chart		

Core quality processes	Process owner	Process target	Acceptable process variation	Process measure	Is the process stable? (Predictable over time) yes or no	Is the process capable? (Ability to meet or exceed expectations) yes or no
Promotion	SF	100% process compliance		Timeline and step checklist		
Reading services (3–5)	CB	100% process compliance After intervention student meets/ exceeds reading RIT growth targets		Timeline and step checklist NWEA typical growth to actual growth		
Report card	RC	100% process compliance		Timeline and step checklist		
Retention	SF/TP	100% process compliance 90% parent satisfaction with placement		Timeline and step checklist Interview or survey XmR chart		
Student acceleration	KF	100% process compliance for step IIA and step IIB 90% placement agreement by consultation meeting participants		Timeline and step checklist for step IIA and step IIB Recorded placement consultation meeting agreement		
Section 504 referral	TP	100% step 1 and 2 compliance 95% step 2 accuracy	No variation acceptable + or − 1 standard deviation	Timeline and step checklist (all) NP chart		
Special education referral	TP	100% step 1 and 2 compliance 95% step 2 accuracy	No variation acceptable + or − 1 standard deviation	Timeline and step checklist (all) NP chart		
Special education services referral (private)	TP	100% step 1 and 2 compliance 95% step 2 accuracy	No variation acceptable + or − 5%	Timeline and step checklist (all) NP chart		

Bibliography

Abbott, J. C. 1999. *SPC: Practical Understanding of Capability by Implementing Statistical Process Control.* Easley, SC: Robert Houston Smith.

American Educational Research Association. 2004. *Research Points* 2, no. 1 (Winter).

American Heritage College Dictionary, 3rd ed. 1993. Boston: Houghton Mifflin.

Arthur, J. 2007. *Lean Six Sigma Demystified.* New York: McGraw Hill.

Baldrige National Quality Program. 2009–2010. *Education Criteria for Performance Excellence.* Milwaukee: ASQ Quality Press.

Blazey, M. L. 2009. *Insights to Performance Excellence 2009–2010: An Inside Look at the 2009–2010 Baldrige Award Criteria.* Milwaukee: ASQ Quality Press.

Deming, W. E. 1982. *Out of the Crisis.* Cambridge, MA: MIT Press.

———. 2000. *The New Economics for Industry, Government, and Education.* Cambridge, MA: MIT Press.

Executive Learning, Inc. 1995. *Continual Improvement Handbook: A Quick Reference Guide for Quality Schools.* Nashville, TN: Executive Learning.

George, M. L., D. Rowlands, M. Price, and J. Maxey. 2005. *The Lean Six Sigma Pocket Toolbook.* New York: McGraw-Hill.

Grayson Jr., C. Jackson. 2009. *The Achilles Heel of Education and How to Fix It.* (White paper.) Houston, TX: American Productivity and Quality Center.

Gygi, C. D., N. DeCarlo, and B. Williams 2005. *Six Sigma for Dummies.* Hoboken: John Wiley & Sons.

Harry, M. S., and R. Schroeder. 2000. *Six Sigma: The Breakthrough Management Strategy Revolutionizing the World's Top Corporations.* New York: Doubleday.

Haynes, R. M., and D. M. Chalker. 1997. *World Class Elementary Schools: Agenda for Action.* Lancaster, PA: Technomic Publishing Company.

Hoerl, R., and R. Snee. 2002. *Statistical Thinking: Improving Business Performance.* Pacific Grove, CA: Duxbury Press.

Jenkins, L. 2003. *Improving Student Learning: Applying Deming's Quality Principles in Classrooms,* 2nd ed. Milwaukee: ASQ Quality Press.

———. 2005. *Permission to Forget.* Milwaukee: ASQ Quality Press.

Joyce, B., and M. Weil. 2008. *Models of Teaching,* 8th ed. New York: Allyn and Bacon.

Juran, J. M., and A. B. Godfrey. 1998. *Juran's Quality Handbook,* 5th ed. New York: McGraw-Hill Professional.

Leonard, J. F. 1996. *The New Philosophy for K–12 Education: A Deming Framework for Transforming America's Schools.* Milwaukee: ASQ Quality Press.

Marzano, R. J. 2003. *What Works in Schools.* Alexandria, VA: Association for Supervision and Curriculum Development.

———. 2007. *The Art and Science of Teaching.* Alexandria, VA: Association for Supervision and Curriculum Development.

Marzano, R. J., D. J. Pickering, and J. E. Pollock. 2001. *Classroom Instruction That Works.* Alexandria, VA: Association for Supervision and Curriculum Development.

Miller, K. 2006. *We Don't Make Widgets: Overcoming the Myths That Keep Government from Radically Improving.* Washington D.C.: Governing Books.

Murphy, C., and D. Lick. 2001. *Whole-Faculty Study Groups: Creating Professional Learning Communities That Target Student Learning.* Thousand Oaks, CA: Corwin Press.

PQ Systems. (1998) *Koalaty Kid Total Quality Tools.* Cincinnati, OH. The Merten Company.

Shewhart, W. A. 1939. *Statistical Method from the Viewpoint of Quality Control.* Washington D.C.: Department of Agriculture.

Steer, Leslie. 2001. "Process Ownership: Great Concept, But What Does It Mean?" *The Human Element* 18, no. 2 (Spring). Milwaukee: ASQ Human Development and Leadership Division.

Tague, N. R. 2005. *The Quality Toolbox,* 2nd ed. Milwaukee: ASQ Quality Press.

U.S. Department of Education home page. Available at: http://www.ed.gov/index.jhtml. Accessed August 10, 2009.

Wheeler, D. J. 2003. *Making Sense of Data: SPC for the Service Sector.* Knoxville, TN: SPC Press.

About the Authors

Robert W. Ewy

504-831-2374
robertewy@cox.net

Robert is currently a consultant in strategic planning, continuous improvement, and process management, assisting school districts that are serious about creating exceptional learning environments for students and satisfying professional working environments for staff. He was most recently the director of planning and quality programs for Community Consolidated School District 15, in Palatine, Illinois. In this role, he was responsible for all aspects of organizational improvement, from the classroom to the boardroom. Robert introduced the Baldrige Criteria to the district and trained board members, all administrators, the professional teaching staff, and support staff in the principles and practices of continuous improvement. Robert was also responsible for all strategic planning activities and for the development and management of assessment processes and the district education data warehouse. He was the primary author of two state and two national Baldrige applications. The second state application won the highest recognition from the Lincoln Foundation for Performance Excellence and the second national Baldrige application resulted in the 2003 Baldrige Award for District 15, the only educational organization to win the award that year and one of five school districts in the nation to ever win the award.

Prior to his District 15 experience, Robert worked for the Mid-Continent Research for Education and Learning (McREL) in Aurora, Colorado, as a senior associate. During his time there, McREL developed a national reputation for developing practical materials for all segments of education that bridged gaps between educational research and practice. Robert was also a supervisor of three statewide school improvement projects for the Colorado Department of Education, a federal programs coordinator for a seven-school district cooperative, and a high school social science teacher.

As a consultant, he most often works with senior leaders to develop or refine strategic plans, deploy plans, align organizational systems, develop process management and improvement methodology, develop assessment metrics, build district-level scorecards, and apply continuous process improvement principles and practices.

Robert has been an Illinois Lincoln Foundation examiner, a senior examiner, and an application judge. He is currently on the board of directors, is the lead judge, and trains examiners for the Louisiana Quality Foundation. He has coauthored a book published by

ASQ Quality Press titled *Charting Your Course: Lessons Learned During the Journey Toward Performance Excellence* and authored *Stakeholder-Driven Strategic Planning in Education: A Practical Guide for Developing and Deploying Successful Long-Range Plans*, both of which have been ASQ best sellers. He has written or contributed to articles about data warehousing and analysis and the principles and practices of continuous improvement.

Henry (Hank) A. Gmitro, EdD

Hank Gmitro has served for 13 years as the superintendent of schools in Community Consolidated School District 93, which serves portions of Carol Stream, Bloomingdale, and Hanover Park, Illinois. Hank began his career as a special education teacher in DeKalb, Illinois. He has also worked as an elementary classroom teacher, a building principal, and an assistant superintendent for instructional services in DeKalb, Glenview, and Palatine, Illinois. During his tenure at CCSD93, the district received the Silver Level Recognition from the Lincoln Foundation for Performance Excellence.

Hank received his bachelor's degree in special education and elementary education from Northern Illinois University. His master's degree in educational administration is also from NIU. Hank completed his doctoral work at the University of Illinois at Urbana–Champaign where his dissertation focused on transformational leadership in the principalship.

In addition to his school district responsibilities, Hank has contributed to the field of education as:

- A current member of the AASA Governing Board

- Chairperson of the DuPage County division of IASA for two years

- Liaison between DuPage IASA and IASB

- Examiner for the Malcolm Baldrige National Quality Award for organizational excellence

- Judge and examiner for the Lincoln Foundation in Illinois

- Chairperson of LEND (The Legislative Educational Network of DuPage)

- A member of numerous national, state, and local committees that promote and support high-quality educational programs for the communities we serve

Index

program solutions, versus process management, 4

Q

QI Macros, 53
quality process examples, Community Consolidated School District 93
K–2 literacy intervention programs, 57
math intervention program, 61
retention procedures, 67
section 504 referral and evaluation procedures, 65
stranger danger, 69
student referral for special education services, 63
Quality Toolbox, The, 53
quality tools, that process manager must master, 38–44

R

Reeves, Douglas, 80, 81, 82
results compared to benchmarks data, 11–12
run chart, 15–16

S

Sanders, William L., 71
school customers, example (Appendix A), 89
shape, of data, 11–12
Shewhart, Walter, 13
"should be" flowchart, 40–41
sigma level, comparisons, 49
SIPOC diagram, 11
Six Sigma, methodology, 47–53
SmartDraw, 26
special causes, of variation, 14, 33, 43
in process improvement, 29
spread, of data, 11–12
square root sampling, 76, 87
stability, process, 6–7, 27, 29, 30, 31–34, 35
in process improvement, 44
standard deviation, 33
statistical process control (SPC), 27, 38–39, 41–44

Statistical Thinking to Improve Quality blog, 5
Standards-Based Instructional Process
flowchart, 71–76
matrix, 83–85
world-class educational practices applied to (classroom focus), 76–78
world-class educational practices applied to (school focus), 78–83
systems, versus processes, 1

T

trend data, 11–12

U

United States Department of Education, goals for education reform, ix–x
upper specification limit (USL), 18

V

value added research, 71
variation
quantification of, 9
sources of, additive property of, 9, 14
variation, of processes, 8–11
and process design, 26
significance of, 5–6
Visio, 26

W

We Don't Make Widgets: Overcoming the Myths That Keep Government from Radically Improving, 4–5
What Works in Schools, 79, 80, 81, 82
White, Michael, 76
Whole-Faculty Study Groups, 83
World Class Elementary Schools, 79

X

XmR chart, 13

Belong to the Quality Community!

Established in 1946, ASQ is a global community of quality experts in all fields and industries. ASQ is dedicated to the promotion and advancement of quality tools, principles, and practices in the workplace and in the community.

The Society also serves as an advocate for quality. Its members have informed and advised the U.S. Congress, government agencies, state legislatures, and other groups and individuals worldwide on quality-related topics.

Vision

By making quality a global priority, an organizational imperative, and a personal ethic, ASQ becomes the community of choice for everyone who seeks quality technology, concepts, or tools to improve themselves and their world.

ASQ is...

- More than 90,000 individuals and 700 companies in more than 100 countries

- The world's largest organization dedicated to promoting quality

- A community of professionals striving to bring quality to their work and their lives

- The administrator of the Malcolm Baldrige National Quality Award

- A supporter of quality in all sectors including manufacturing, service, healthcare, government, and education

- YOU

ASQ

Visit www.asq.org for more information.

ASQ Membership

Research shows that people who join associations experience increased job satisfaction, earn more, and are generally happier*. ASQ membership can help you achieve this while providing the tools you need to be successful in your industry and to distinguish yourself from your competition. So why wouldn't you want to be a part of ASQ?

Networking

Have the opportunity to meet, communicate, and collaborate with your peers within the quality community through conferences and local ASQ section meetings, ASQ forums or divisions, ASQ Communities of Quality discussion boards, and more.

Professional Development

Access a wide variety of professional development tools such as books, training, and certifications at a discounted price. Also, ASQ certifications and the ASQ Career Center help enhance your quality knowledge and take your career to the next level.

Solutions

Find answers to all your quality problems, big and small, with ASQ's Knowledge Center, mentoring program, various e-newsletters, *Quality Progress* magazine, and industry-specific products.

Access to Information

Learn classic and current quality principles and theories in ASQ's Quality Information Center (QIC), *ASQ Weekly* e-newsletter, and product offerings.

Advocacy Programs

ASQ helps create a better community, government, and world through initiatives that include social responsibility, Washington advocacy, and Community Good Works.

Visit www.asq.org/membership for more information on ASQ membership.

*2008, The William E. Smith Institute for Association Research

ASQ Certification

ASQ certification is formal recognition by ASQ that an individual has demonstrated a proficiency within, and comprehension of, a specified body of knowledge at a point in time. Nearly 150,000 certifications have been issued. ASQ has members in more than 100 countries, in all industries, and in all cultures. ASQ certification is internationally accepted and recognized.

Benefits to the Individual

- New skills gained and proficiency upgraded
- Investment in your career
- Mark of technical excellence
- Assurance that you are current with emerging technologies
- Discriminator in the marketplace
- Certified professionals earn more than their uncertified counterparts
- Certification is endorsed by more than 125 companies

Benefits to the Organization

- Investment in the company's future
- Certified individuals can perfect and share new techniques in the workplace
- Certified staff are knowledgeable and able to assure product and service quality

Quality is a global concept. It spans borders, cultures, and languages. No matter what country your customers live in or what language they speak, they demand quality products and services. You and your organization also benefit from quality tools and practices. Acquire the knowledge to position yourself and your organization ahead of your competition.

Certifications Include

- Biomedical Auditor – CBA
- Calibration Technician – CCT
- HACCP Auditor – CHA
- Pharmaceutical GMP Professional – CPGP
- Quality Inspector – CQI
- Quality Auditor – CQA
- Quality Engineer – CQE
- Quality Improvement Associate – CQIA
- Quality Technician – CQT
- Quality Process Analyst – CQPA
- Reliability Engineer – CRE
- Six Sigma Black Belt – CSSBB
- Six Sigma Green Belt – CSSGB
- Software Quality Engineer – CSQE
- Manager of Quality/Organizational Excellence – CMQ/OE

Visit www.asq.org/certification to apply today!

ASQ Training

Classroom-based Training

ASQ offers training in a traditional classroom setting on a variety of topics. Our instructors are quality experts and lead courses that range from one day to four weeks, in several different cities. Classroom-based training is designed to improve quality and your organization's bottom line. Benefit from quality experts; from comprehensive, cutting-edge information; and from peers eager to share their experiences.

Web-based Training

Virtual Courses

ASQ's virtual courses provide the same expert instructors, course materials, interaction with other students, and ability to earn CEUs and RUs as our classroom-based training, without the hassle and expenses of travel. Learn in the comfort of your own home or workplace. All you need is a computer with Internet access and a telephone.

Self-paced Online Programs

These online programs allow you to work at your own pace while obtaining the quality knowledge you need. Access them whenever it is convenient for you, accommodating your schedule.

Some Training Topics Include

- Auditing
- Basic Quality
- Engineering
- Education
- Healthcare
- Government
- Food Safety
- ISO
- Leadership
- Lean
- Quality Management
- Reliability
- Six Sigma
- Social Responsibility

Visit www.asq.org/training for more information.